From bitter to sweet

John Currid

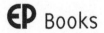 Books

EP Books
Faverdale North, Darlington, DL3 0PH, England

web: www.epbooks.org
email: sales@epbooks.org

First published 2012

British Library Cataloguing in Publication Data available
ISBN-13 978 085234 788 1

Printed and bound in the UK by the MPG Books Group

To
Professor Knox Chamblin
(1935–2012)

Contents

Introduction

The book of Ruth is a wonderful short story. Many people throughout the ages have been touched by the sweetness and kindness so evident in the episode. Even Thomas Paine, the ardent rationalist, recognized its special nature:

> The book of Ruth, an idle, bungling story, foolishly told, nobody knows by whom, about a strolling country girl, creeping slyly to be with her cousin Boaz. Pretty stuff indeed, to be called the Word of God! It is, however, one of the best books of the Bible, for it is free from murder and rapine.[1]

Although Paine's details about, and understanding of, the book are skewed, he does acknowledge its unique nature as having occurred during the period of the judges, when violence reigned in Israel. Ruth has none of that ferocity and turmoil.

People have also been drawn to the book because it is a most beautiful love story. It is common in modern marriage ceremonies to include a quote of Ruth 1:16: 'Do not urge me to leave you or to return from following you. For where you go I will go, and where you lodge I will lodge. Your people shall be my people, and your God my God.' The book of Ruth has even been called an ancient 'biblical Cinderella story' in which Ruth finds her true prince by the close of the tale. It is thus viewed almost as a rags-to-riches fairy tale.

Although the human relationships in the story are encouraging to us and the characters are worthy of emulation in some ways, these aspects are hardly the main point of the book. How the people deal with one another, their kindness to each other and their upright characters belong in the first tier of interpretation. We must go deeper and wider to understand truly the purpose and meaning of the writing.

A second tier of interpretation arises from an in-depth study of the text. The time of Ruth is the period of the judges, and it is characterized as one in which 'there was no king in Israel' (Judg. 21:25). The book of Ruth, however, anticipates the coming of a great king to the throne of Israel. It records the ancestry of David, the most beloved king in the history of Israel. Thus, in one sense, the account finds its climax and zenith in the coming of David, whose ancestors are Ruth and Boaz. Thus the book is serving a greater purpose than merely being a moral story of human goodness: it points to a future reality of the coming of the king.

Yet the eventual arrival of David is not the final or ultimate climax of the book. In reality, the narrative reaches its crescendo in the coming of the last and consummate king, who is Christ Jesus, the son of David. Indeed, many of the main characters of the book of Ruth are listed as ancestors of Jesus in his genealogy (Matt. 1:1-17). This is the highest tier of meaning in the story, and the reader ought to keep it in mind continually when studying the book. The great end of the story is the glorious and wondrous coming of the Messiah!

Date and authorship

The writer of the book of Ruth is anonymous. This fact, however, has not dulled speculation over the question of its authorship.

If anything, it has increased the number of proposals that have been presented. Much ink has been spilled over this most enigmatic issue. A widely held position today is that Solomon wrote the book after the death of his father David.[2] The Babylonian Talmud treatise called *Baba Bathra* considers the prophet Samuel as the author: 'Samuel wrote his book, Judges, and Ruth.' In support of this attribution, some commentators argue that Ruth was originally part of the book of Judges, and so both books must be by the same author. There is, however, little evidence for such a connection, although Josephus was perhaps the first to believe that Ruth is attached to Judges. Later writers, such as Origen and Jerome, agree that the two books are to be read together. Other modern commentators argue that Ruth was composed by a writer known as the 'Deuteronomist', who did his work in the post-exilic period of the fifth century BC. Some suggest that the storyteller is female because of the prominence of women in the book. Who knows? All of this appears to be an exercise in futility.

The earliest possible date that the book of Ruth could have been written is in the time of David, because the account ends with a genealogy in which his name is the final entry. David's accession to the throne of Judah occurred around 1010 BC, and he ruled over Judah, and later over a united Israel, until *c.* 970 BC. The author, therefore, wrote the book during or after this time. He probably employed written ancestral records and an oral history which had been related to him.

Key themes

1. The cost of disobedience

The people of God need to understand that there are consequences to their sin. Although believers have been delivered from sin by the work of Christ, there are nevertheless

9

temporal results to our disobedience to God and his word. Elimelech and his family belong to the people of God, yet, when hardship strikes, they move to Moab. They place themselves under Moabite authority, and the two sons of the family even marry foreign women. This activity ends up in poverty, widowhood and, ultimately, death.

2. God's sovereignty

God's providence shines forth even in the midst of man's sin and disobedience. Through the move of Elimelech's family to Moab, we witness God's sovereign, unconditional election of Ruth as a believer. She is an heir of salvation. This story, then, is a picture of the engrafting of the Gentiles into the people of God. The fact that Ruth herself is included in the genealogy of Jesus confirms that truth (Matt. 1:5). God's sovereignty is further revealed throughout the book in many ways as he preserves the line of the Messiah; that is not left to chance, but God is working, guiding and directing.

3. Faithful living

Boaz and Ruth are characters of faith, and they are persons of integrity, industry and honour. They exhibit their faith in the way they live and act. Their conduct is a true reflection of their faith as followers of the Lord.

4. Redemption

The biblical concept of redemption is at the very heart of the story. Redemption is a Hebrew cultural practice in which something that has been alienated might be restored to a family by a kinsman-redeemer, or next of kin. Thus, if a person has to sell himself or his land to pay a debt, then the kinsman-redeemer has the duty to step in and act upon the situation. He is to redeem and to restore. As one can imagine, there are varied circumstances with regard to these laws, and the book of Ruth presents customs applicable to the period of the judges. Most importantly, the Hebrew customs of redemption are a picture of God's relationship to, and activity on behalf of, his covenant people. This latter truth will be fleshed out as we work our way through the text.

Outline

The book of Ruth is outlined in the following fashion:

Act I: **Setting the scene** (1:1-5)

Act II: **Naomi and her Moabite daughters-in-law**
(1:622)
Scene 1: Graciousness in the midst of suffering (1:6-9)
Scene 2: Orpah and Ruth respond (1:10-14)
Scene 3: Ruth's confession (1:15-18)
Scene 4: Homecoming (1:19-22)

Act III: **In the fields of Bethlehem** (2:1-23)
Scene 1: Ruth gleans in the fields (2:1-7)
Scene 2: Conversations between Ruth and Boaz (2:817)
Scene 3: Ruth reports to Naomi (2:18-23)

Act IV: **The scene at the threshing floor** (3:1-18)
Scene 1: Naomi's plan (3:1-6)
Scene 2: At the threshing floor (3:7-13)
Scene 3: Back to Bethlehem (3:14-18)

Act V: **Redemption** (4:1-22)
Scene 1: The courtroom scene (4:1-12)
Scene 2: The descendant (4:13-22)

The book begins by laying out the background and setting of the story. It tells us that these events are set in the period of the judges, which is properly understood as a degenerate time in the history of Israel. This introduction, however, centres on one particular family during this period, and how they cope with the hardship of famine. It describes the family's move to the country of Moab.

The second section narrates the return to Israel of Naomi, the mother of the family, along with one of her daughters-in-law named Ruth. They are both widows and, therefore, suffering great affliction. They are confronted with the issue of survival.

Ruth, in the third part, labours in the fields of Bethlehem in order to provide for her mother-in-law and herself. There she gleans in the fields of a man named Boaz. Boaz is a kinsman-redeemer of the family of Elimelech. Ruth and Boaz meet and they have a series of conversations with one another. He is particularly kind to her.

Naomi hatches a plan to move Boaz to act on his status as kinsman-redeemer with regard to her family's land and to Ruth. This constitutes the fourth section of the book. Ruth secretly meets Boaz at the threshing floor, and there he promises to act the part of the kinsman-redeemer on her behalf.

Finally, the book ends on a high note. The section begins with a courtroom scene in which Boaz lays out his case for redemption. All matters go his way, and he ends up marrying Ruth and serving as kinsman-redeemer for her and for Elimelech's holdings. Ruth bears a son who becomes an ancestor of David, the great king of Israel. The section ends with a genealogy that traces David's ancestry from Perez down through Boaz.

Now let us turn to the text itself, and let us attempt to understand its wonderful and gripping message.

12

Part 1:
Setting the scene (1:1-5)

Chapter 1
The setting of suffering

Please read Ruth 1:1-5

Maintaining a steadfast trust in God in all circumstances is a difficult thing to do. Early in his days of ministry, John Wesley travelled from London to Georgia in the New World. There he hoped to minister among the Indians and settlers, and he desired to see many conversions among the people. His ministry did not go well. As Dallimore remarks, 'He was in bitter dejection, for his whole person was shaken by the realization that salvation was not to be gained by any programme of human effort.' He fled back to England and confessed, 'What have I learned? Why, what I the least of suspected, that I who went to America to convert others, was never myself converted to God.'[1]

Wesley witnessed this steadfast trust in the lives of the Moravians, a German evangelical group. At sea when the ship was hit by a violent storm he noticed that 'a terrible screaming began among the English'. The Moravians, however — men, women, and children — calmly sang a hymn of trust and praise. Wesley was startled because he realized that these Christians possessed something he did not have, and he admitted during the storm, 'I was afraid to die.' Later, the Moravian leaders continued to ply Wesley with questions, such as, 'Do you know Jesus Christ?' and 'Do you know if he has saved your soul?'

These were Wesley's first contacts with evangelical Christianity and 'they left a lasting mark'.

A Christian's life should be characterized by a continual desire for greater trust in God. John Newton's letter to a certain Captain Clunie, dated 12 October 1776, reflects this well:

> I long to have a more entire submission to his will, and a more steadfast confidence in his word, to trust him and wait on him, to see his hand and praise his name in every circumstance of life great and small. The more of this spirit, the more heaven is begun upon earth. And why should we not trust him at all times? Which part of our past experience can charge him with unfaithfulness? Has he not done all things well? And is he not the same yesterday, today, and for ever? O my soul, wait thou only upon him.

At the outset of the book of Ruth we are confronted with an Israelite family that is in dire economic straits. The question is, how will this family respond to these difficult times? In what will they put their trust?

The backdrop (1:1)

The book begins with the words: *'In the days when the judges ruled...'* This expression provides the timing and background of the story: it occurs during the period that is described in the book of Judges. In general, what do we know about this period of history? The last verse of the book of Judges is a summary statement that encapsulates the aura of the times: 'In those days there was no king in Israel. Everyone did what was right in his own eyes' (Judg. 21:25). That thematic statement reflects a state of political anarchy. There is a distinct lack of a central political authority in Israel at this time. But this description is also one that indicates a lack of spiritual focus. There exists a dominant relativism. This relativism violates God's covenant in two significant ways. First, God's covenant law is no longer the standard; rather, the people are doing what is best in their own eyes. Secondly, the unity intended among Israel as God's covenant people has broken down into individualism. People are simply trusting in themselves.

Some time during the period of the judges there occurs 'a famine in the land'. In other words, some type of economic and agricultural adversity strikes the covenant people in the land of promise. Famine in Israel was a calamity that commonly befell the inhabitants of the land in biblical times. For example, Abraham flees to Egypt as a result of a famine in Canaan (Gen. 12:10). Jacob brings the Hebrew people to Egypt from Canaan because of a particularly severe famine (Gen. 42 – 47). Often in the Old Testament a famine is understood as a sign of God's displeasure with an unfaithful Israel. Leviticus 26:18-20, for instance, quotes God speaking to Israel:

> And if in spite of this you will not listen to me, then I will discipline you again sevenfold for your sins, and I will break the pride of your power, and I will make your heavens like iron and your earth like bronze. And your strength shall be spent in vain, for your land shall not yield its increase, and the trees of the land shall not yield their fruit.

Of course, the period of the judges was a time of Israel's overall disobedience and unfaithfulness and, therefore, it is not surprising that a famine came on the land (cf. Amos 8:11-12). These were difficult times for God's people; it was a period

17

of moral collapse, great apostasy and physical hardship. How would the people of Israel respond to such adversity?

The book of Ruth begins as a story of what one man does in the midst of the famine. The text describes this person as *a man of Bethlehem in Judah.* Where the man comes from is important to the story.

First, the name of his home town underscores a bitter irony: the famine hits the town of Bethlehem, a name that literally means 'the house of bread', or 'the house of food'.

Secondly, the town is identified with the tribe of Judah, and that distinguishes it from another Bethlehem, which belongs to the tribe of Zebulun (Josh. 19:15-16). To the reader, both ancient and modern, the town of Bethlehem in Judah should immediately bring to mind that this was the home town of David, the great king of Israel. And, of course, the New Testament records that it was also the birthplace of the coming Messianic king, the Son of David (Matt. 2:1). Irony again plays into the story: at the time of the judges there was no king in Israel, yet the story of Ruth is set in the very place where the greatest kings in Israel's history will be born.

This man from Bethlehem in Judah takes his immediate family and leaves the land of promise to 'sojourn' in the land of Moab. 'Sojourning' is a technical term used in antiquity for a person who is living as an alien in a foreign land. It describes the social standing of someone who works in a foreign country but has few of the rights and privileges of citizenship. One who sojourns does not own land, but is generally in the service of a native who is his or her master and protector. Thus, this man from Bethlehem leaves the lands allotted to his tribe and clan in Israel to put himself in a position paramount to servitude in a foreign land.

What do we know about Moab at this time? First, the Moabites were descendants of Lot; the person named Moab, who was the progenitor of this people, was born as a result of incest between Lot and one of his daughters (Gen. 19:37). Their habitation was on the east side of the Jordan River. The Moabites were pagan, and their main god was Chemosh (Num. 21:29). They also worshipped the notorious god Baal of Peor (Num. 25:1-3). During the period of the judges, in which the book of Ruth takes place, the Moabites were arch-enemies of Israel (see, in particular, Judg. 3:12-30).

One wonders whether this Israelite man does the right thing by abandoning his ancestral holdings and going to Moab to serve under pagan authority. I believe we can understand his reasoning — that is, he is concerned for the economic well-being of his family. On the other hand, as the story unfolds it appears that the man is actually putting his family in harm's way, rather than trusting in God's provision for them in the land of promise. The reality is that not all Israel responds in the way that this man does; many, like Boaz, remain in the land awaiting God's provision for them.

In any event, this man leaves Israel for Moab, and he takes his wife and two sons with him. Apparently neither son is married at this time.

The names of the characters (1:2)

Names of people in the Old Testament may be an integral part of the story being told.

The naming of a child may *reflect an important event in the life of the nation or family.* Thus, for instance, the name Isaac

19

means 'laughter', and that term is a dominant motif in the birth narrative of Isaac. In Genesis 17:17 Abraham laughed when told that Sarah would bear a child in old age. Sarah herself laughed at the thought of it (Gen. 18:12). And in Genesis 21:6, Sarah claims that everyone who hears of the unique birth of Isaac will laugh.

The naming of a person may be *anticipatory*. Abel's name, for example, means 'fleeting', or 'vapour', and, indeed, it reflects his short-lived existence.

Some names are directly *prophetic*. Isaiah called his son Maher-shalal-hashbaz, which means, 'Swift is the booty, speedy is the prey' (Isa. 8:1-4). His naming is a prophecy of the coming Assyrian army's invasion of Israel.

Names, therefore, can sometimes be a key to unlocking an important truth or motif in a story. This is the case in the book of Ruth.

The name of the man from Bethlehem in Judah is *'Elimelech'*, which literally means, 'My God is king.' That proper name is ironic considering the nature of the period of the judges, in which 'there was no king in Israel. Everyone did what was right in his own eyes' (Judg. 21:25). In reality, not even God was king in Israel at this time, and this man is a testimony to the tenor of the period; he was doing what was right in his own eyes by leaving Israel and becoming a resident alien in Moab.

The name of the man's wife is *'Naomi'*, which in Hebrew derives from a word that means 'sweet, pleasant, delightful'.[2] Later in the chapter Naomi will change her name to a word that will reflect the opposite of her given name, describing her as one who is in desperate circumstances (see comments on 1:19-21).

20

The name of their older son is 'Mahlon'. The meaning of this name is uncertain, although it may be related to a word that means 'sickly, weak, ill'. The second son is 'Chilion', which derives from a term that means 'failing or pining away'.[3] Although we cannot be certain, it may be that the two names of the sons anticipate the deaths that will soon come upon them.

This family belongs to the Judahite clan of the 'Ephrathites' which is centred on the village of Bethlehem. Again, the reader is to be reminded at this point of King David. Early in the account of David's life, we read, 'Now David was the son of an Ephrathite of Bethlehem in Judah' (1 Sam. 17:12). As we shall see repeatedly through the book of Ruth, the narrative is driving towards David with great clarity. In a time when there was no king in Israel, this book anticipates the kingship of David.

At the close of the verse, the family travels to Moab and they become resident aliens in that foreign land.

Dire straits (1:3)

The family is under great hardship. There is a famine in Israel, and so they go to sojourn in Moab and to live there under the authority of the pagan Moabites. Tragedy then strikes: Elimelech, the husband of Naomi, dies. Thus, matters are moving from bad to worse. Naomi is now a widow. Nevertheless not all is bleak, because she still has her two sons to care for her; she is not yet destitute.

One can imagine how difficult and heartbreaking the death of her husband would have been for Naomi. Numerous psychological studies today tell us that one of the most trying and difficult periods in a person's life is the loss of a spouse.

21

Many of these studies rank it as the second most difficult event that many people have to face. What is often ranked as the greatest hardship in life? We need not wait long to get the answer to that question, for in two verses' time Naomi will endure that as well.

Life goes on (1:4)

When God's people go through trials and tribulations, they often glean comfort from the doctrine of the providence of God. In other words, if one of God's people is enduring hardship, it is because this fits into God's overall plan for that person's life. A confirming verse in this regard is Romans 8:28: 'And we know that for those who love God all things work together for good, for those who are called according to his purpose.' This is true doctrine. If it happens, it is due to providence and it is brought about by the sovereign hand of God.

However, we need to be careful not to conclude, when hard things happen to us, that we are mere victims of providence or circumstance. The reality is that adversity often comes because of the way that we think, act and behave. For example, when Moses murders an Egyptian, he is forced to flee Egypt and then endure hardship in the desert for forty years (Exod. 2:11-22). Moses reaps temporal consequences for his sinful activity. On the other hand, the Lord uses such shameful activity to bring about his good purposes. In that desert of hardship, God prepares Moses to shepherd his people through that very same barren land. This reality may be summarized by Joseph's statement to his brothers after they had sinfully sold him into Egypt: 'As for you, you meant evil against me, but God meant it for good, to bring it about that many people should be kept alive, as they are today' (Gen. 50:20).

May we grasp the truth that God will use his people despite their sin. That, of course, does not give anyone a licence to sin, but it underscores the reality that God employs frail and weak vessels to proclaim his truth. God uses his people, despite their feebleness, debility and transgressions, for his glory and purposes.

This is what happens in the book of Ruth. As has already been suggested, the act of Elimelech to move his family to Moab because of a famine in Israel was not the right response to adversity. He should have trusted in the Lord's provision and remained steadfast in the land of his inheritance. Now in verse 4 we see another errant action: Naomi's two Hebrew sons marry Moabite women. How often biblical law demands that the Israelites should not intermarry with pagan peoples! Deuteronomy 7:3-4, for example, says, 'You shall not intermarry with them, giving your daughters to their sons or taking their daughters for your sons, for they would turn away your sons from following me, to serve other gods.' Yet, as we shall see, the sovereign God will even take such sinful activity and redeem it for his own glory and purposes. The characters in the story do suffer temporal hardships because of their sin, yet all will end up to the glory of God.

The names of the two Moabite wives are provided in verse 4. The first daughter-in-law is 'Orpah'. The meaning of her name is disputed. Some argue that it means 'to be stiff-necked or stubborn', and others that it refers to 'a girl with a full mane'.[4] The second daughter-in-law is 'Ruth'. Many commentators agree that her name derives from a root that signifies 'friendship', or 'companionship'.[5]

This extended family, now lacking the leadership of Elimelech, becomes entrenched in the land of Moab, having settled there

23

for approximately ten years. Warning bells ought to be ringing. Certainly over this extended time period, acculturation and assimilation to Moabite culture would have been a constant danger and threat to these Israelites. It is reminiscent in some ways of Lot's absorption into Sodomite culture so clearly portrayed in Genesis 13 – 19. Lot moved to Sodom, and he became a property owner, a townsman, and perhaps married one of the native population. His daughters married Sodomites (Gen. 19:14). All of that led to disaster.

Increase of adversity (1:5)

Perhaps the greatest hardship that people ever face is the loss of a child. Naomi loses both of her sons after the death of her husband. This is heart-wrenching; yet it is perhaps even more severe than we realize. Naomi's situation is grave: she is now a widow with no sons to care for her. Certainly the Moabites would have no sense of responsibility for the widow of a sojourner; Naomi would have very few rights and privileges in that culture. So, on top of her grief and mourning, Naomi is facing destitution, poverty, and perhaps even enslavement. The latter would appear to be her only option in Moab unless she were to marry a Moabite. Marriage for Naomi is unlikely (see 1:12). The reality is that she is in a hopeless, desperate situation as she faces some of the great miseries of life. *What will she do?*

Difficult circumstances ought to lead a child of God into a period of self-examination. They ought to cause one to assess how one is living before God on this earth. The Puritan commentator Matthew Henry says in this regard, 'When death comes into a family it ought to be improved [i.e. made good use of] for the reforming of what is amiss in the family.' Such tragedy as Naomi is facing ought to lead to change, and it ought to bring

24

into focus the things that are truly important. For Naomi, this change is about to take place.

Points to ponder

In the middle of the eighteenth century in America, a certain young man was attending Yale University as a full-time divinity student. His desire was to be trained for the pastoral ministry. He was an excellent student, and after a few years of hard study he was close to completing his work. However, one day an unfortunate incident occurred. The student was talking to some friends and made the unguarded remark about one of his professors: 'That man is about as spiritual as this chair I'm sitting in!'

The student was expelled from Yale. It was a sinful thing he had said, and he later repented and asked the professor for forgiveness. However, he was never readmitted to the divinity school at the university. Thus began what was perhaps the lowest, most depressing and most discouraging period in the life of David Brainerd.

But the Scriptures call us to understand that God uses even our most despicable acts to bring about his good purposes. And so God worked his good pleasure in the life of David Brainerd. After his expulsion from Yale, Brainerd agonized over his calling — but God opened up a service for him on the mission field to the Indians. That had not been Brainerd's desire, but God gave him that desire. And, of course, God blessed his ministry with great revivals among the Indians. God can use even the sin of man to bring about his good purposes for the world. He is simply sovereign, and nothing happens in heaven or on earth apart from his decrees.

Part 2:
Naomi and her Moabite daughters-in-law
(1:6-22)

Chapter 2
Graciousness in the midst of suffering

Please read Ruth 1:6-9

The Lord does not leave his people in adversity indefinitely. There is an end to suffering for the believer, whether it comes here on earth or in heaven (see Isa. 40:28-31). Suffering does not, and will not, gain victory over the Christian. John Newton wrote the following in a letter to a member of his congregation who was undergoing affliction:

> Like sheep, we are weak, destitute, defenceless, prone to wander, unable to return, and always surrounded by wolves. But all is made up in the fullness, ability, wisdom, compassion, care, and faithfulness of our great Shepherd. He guides, protects, feeds, heals, and restores, and will be our guide and our God even until death. Then he will meet us, receive us, and present us unto himself, and we shall be near to him, and like him, and with him for ever.

And, so, in verses 6-9 of Ruth chapter 1, the Lord has mercy and compassion upon his people in the land of Israel: he turns away the famine and provides food for them.

Yahweh visits his people (1:6)

Naomi now makes plans to return to her family's inheritance in the land of promise. There appear to be two main reasons for her return.

First, as we have already seen, Naomi is under no one's protection in the land of Moab. She has no kinsmen in Moab, and as a widow she could easily be taken advantage of. As an aside, this circumstance parallels Ruth's later situation when she first arrives in Israel. Ruth is a sojourner working in the fields, and she is a widow with no male protection. She could easily have been abased and abused in the fields as a pagan, foreign widow! In any event, Naomi's response to her adversity is to return to her people.

German biblical scholars have a name for a word that appears repeatedly throughout a passage. They call it a leitwort, which means 'a leading word', or keyword. A leitwort often provides keen insight into the sense of a passage. In verses 622 of Ruth chapter 1 the verb 'to return' occurs twelve times. While this verb is commonly used in Hebrew of a person changing a course of action and physically returning to a place, it is also often employed of a spiritual renewal. Frequently it is used in the Old Testament for a person who repents and turns back to God (e.g., Hosea 3:5; 6:1; 7:10). So its repeated appearance in our text probably indicates that the characters are not only returning to the land of promise, but they are turning to Yahweh.

The second reason for Naomi to return to Israel is that she has heard that God has visited his people, has ended the famine and is now providing sustenance for them. The famine was the reason why Naomi's family left Israel in the first place, but now it is over. It is important to observe that, as God brought the

30

famine, so he has graciously removed it. These things do not come by nature alone: the text underscores the providence of God in nature by saying, 'The Lord had visited his people and [he had] given them food.' God is the source and cause of the famine, and he is the source and cause of its relief.

It is also important to point out that the Hebrew name for God used in this verse is 'Yahweh'. This is the covenantal name for God that he revealed to Moses at the burning bush (Exod. 3:14). Thus, we see in verse 6 of the present chapter that Yahweh comes to the aid of 'his people': he visits them graciously and provides food for them. The covenant people are singled out as the ones receiving material grace.

Yahweh provides 'food' for his people. This is the same word that is used in verse 1 in the Hebrew compound word 'Bethlehem'. The latter is literally 'the house of food', or 'the house of bread'. God has taken 'bread' away from 'the house of bread' (1:1), and now he provides 'bread' for 'the house of bread' (1:6).

Beginning the journey (1:7)

The three women — Naomi, Orpah and Ruth — begin the trek to Bethlehem in Judah. Both daughters-in-law are dutiful at this point, and they are demonstrating honour and proper respect for their mother-in-law. This is not easy. Naomi's hardship of being a widow and a sojourner will soon become the lot of her daughters-in-law. They will arrive in Israel as widows without male protection and as resident aliens in a foreign land.

It is clear from cultural practices of the ancient Near East and from the text of Ruth 1 that Orpah and Ruth are not required or under any obligation to go with Naomi. They have every

31

right to return to their extended families and clans, and to the protection provided by blood relationships. Why, then, do these two women resolve to set off with Naomi? Why go with her to place themselves in a vulnerable situation? Obviously they love and care for their mother-in-law. What a rare and sweet thing!

This verse gives the specific destination of the women. They are going to 'the land of Judah'. For Naomi, this is a return to her ancestral roots and to the land of her husband Elimelech's inheritance. It is simply time for her to go home.

Naomi's plea (1:8-9)

On the way, Naomi has second thoughts. She turns to her two daughters-in-law and forcefully orders them to return to their Moabite families. She employs two imperatives at the beginning of her speech — literally, 'Go! Return!' Naomi is acting selflessly here. She certainly would be better off with their support and having them as travelling companions. Yet she is gracious. What does she have to give them? She has no sons and no security. She is poverty-stricken. Naomi understands that they would be placing themselves in harm's way if they went with her.

Each young woman would clearly be better off in 'her mother's house'. This is unique language because the extended family in Hebrew is normally referred to as 'the father's house' (Gen. 12:1; 1 Sam. 2:28; 9:20; etc.). Naomi employs the former designation for the family in order to underscore that there is a closer female-to-female relationship, between mother and daughter, than between mother-in-law and daughter-in-law. In addition, there is more safety and security there. Their privileges and rights as citizens would continue. Perhaps the family could

32

secure another marriage for them. The reality is that everything related to the word 'home' awaits these young women if they remain in Moab. There is an easy road and there is a hard road. Naomi is encouraging Orpah and Ruth to take the easy one by going home.

Naomi then pronounces a blessing on the young women. She begins with the oath: '*May the Lord deal kindly with you.*' In this blessing, Naomi invokes the name Yahweh. She is not using some generic name for deity in the ancient Near East, but she is calling on the covenantal name for God in front of, and on behalf of, two Moabite women. This is a wonderful confession and testimony on Naomi's part!

Naomi calls upon Yahweh to '*deal kindly*' with Orpah and Ruth. This is a weighty term in Hebrew (chesed) which is best translated as 'loyalty', or 'covenant loyalty'. She is calling on the covenant God to be loyal to these two Moabite women. There is a sense of redemptive irony in the blessing: as these young women have been loyal to Naomi, may Naomi's God be loyal to them! Naomi is simply entrusting their keeping to the covenant God of Israel, Yahweh.

In verse 9, Naomi calls for a specific and special blessing from Yahweh upon these women. May they '*find rest, each of you in the house of her husband!*' In the previous verse Naomi had called for the women to return 'each ... to her mother's house'. Now she calls for something more — namely, that they would find new husbands and be settled in new families. She further implores that they would find '*rest*' in those new homes. The Hebrew word she uses often refers in the Old Testament to the land of promise — it is the place of repose for the people of God (Deut. 12:9; 1 Kings 8:56; Ps. 23:2).

Finally, there is an emotional and a physical response by all three women. Naomi kisses Orpah and Ruth, and then they all cry out and weep. This, again, is a heart-wrenching affair: Naomi is a sojourner who has lost her husband and her two sons, and now she is about to be bereft of her two daughters-in-law whom she truly loves. But even in the midst of such suffering and bereavement, she pronounces a blessing of God upon others. Naomi's piety and virtue are clearly on display in this passage.

Points to ponder

1. Adversity urges us to Christ

As with Naomi, adversity often has the result of driving the believer back to God. The psalmist declares about Israel that:

> When he [God] killed them, they sought him;
> they repented and sought God earnestly.
> They remembered that God was their rock,
> the Most High God their redeemer. (Ps. 78:34-35)

> Intense afflictions ... are beneficial to the Christian: in earnest, the elect goes into God's presence seeking His help and consolation. One purpose, then, for the Christian under trial is [that] it demonstrates our helplessness and insufficiency to deal with adversity. Believers are simply driven to lean and depend upon God. As Calvin remarks, '... humbled, we learn to call upon his power, which alone makes us stand fast under the weight of afflictions.'[1]

The believer's return to God can come in a variety of forms. Afflictions quicken the believer to prayer. Adversity drives the

34

Christian to the Bible. In hardship, the believer is impelled to turn and lean upon God, who is the only source of true satisfaction and serenity. Thomas Watson explains this purpose of suffering as follows:

> In prosperity the heart is apt to be divided (Hos. 10:2). The heart cleaves partly to God, and partly to the world... God draws and the world draws. Now God takes away the world, that the heart may cleave more to Him in sincerity ... when God sets our worldly comforts on fire, then we run to Him, and make our peace with him.[2]

2. Service in the midst of suffering

Naomi is a great example to us of one who is gracious in the midst of her own suffering. Although she is desperate and dispirited, she nevertheless encourages others — she even calls a blessing on others from her position in the depths of the valley of death and darkness. In this way, she is a great example and witness to the truth of the religion of the God of Israel.

Jesus is, of course, the greatest example of this character trait. Hebrews 2:18 says of Christ, 'For because he himself has suffered when tempted, he is able to help those who are being tempted.' In our process of sanctification — that is, in our becoming more and more like Christ — may we pray that this characteristic of Christ would become our own; so that when we undergo adversity we would not be self-centred and self-involved, but we would serve others, even in the midst of our sufferings. In this regard may we be bright lights of testimony to the truth and power of God in us.

Jonathan Edwards, in his treatise *A Faithful Narrative of Surprising Conversions*, tells the story of Phebe Bartlett, who was

35

born in 1731. At the age of four she was deeply moved by the Spirit, and even at that young age she became serious about her faith. Her parents noticed that she would pray five to six times a day. And on one occasion her mother heard her pray, 'Pray, blessed Lord, give me salvation! I pray, pardon all my sins!' From that day forward there was a deep and lasting change in her life. In December 1804, Phebe travelled to the town of Westhampton with her husband to visit her son. She became quite ill. A certain man named Justin Edwards (no relation to Jonathan) helped to nurse her. He was converted as he saw her face adversity, or, as he said in his own words, he 'saw the dying woman calmly trusting in her Saviour'. He said to himself, 'Here is a religion that I have not, and that I must have.' Phebe Bartlett died of her illness in January 1805. Justin Edwards became a pastor and served for years at the South Church in Andover, Massachusetts. He later became president of Andover Theological Seminary.

The reality is that the truth burned brightly in the life of Phebe Bartlett from the time of her conversion at four years old until her death at the age of seventy-three. She was a faithful witness for Christ from childhood to the tomb. And, indeed, even in adversity she was a witness to Christ. What a great example for us to follow in our walk with Jesus!

Chapter 3
Orpah and Ruth respond

Please read Ruth 1:10-14

It is important at this point in the story that we recognize that foundational to all that is taking place is the sovereignty of God. Naomi, in the present passage, certainly acknowledges the truth of this doctrine (1:13). A. W. Pink defines God's sovereignty as follows:

> The sovereignty of God may be defined as the exercise of His supremacy... God does as He pleases, only as He pleases, always as He pleases... Divine sovereignty means that God in fact, as well as in name, that He is on the throne of the universe directing all things, working all things 'after the counsel of His own will' (Eph. 1:11).[1]

Thus, while we are intent on understanding and learning the human story in the book of Ruth, we should also take great care that we do not miss how this human story fits into God's grand scheme of redemption. Indeed, the bigger and more important story is the unfolding of redemptive history according to God's decree and design.

Naomi truly understands that everything that has come upon her proceeds from the hand of God. Whether good or bad, it ultimately derives from him. E. B. Pusey gets to the heart of this truth when he says:

> This, then, is of faith, that everything, the very least, or what seems to us great, every change of the seasons, everything that touches us in mind, body, or estate, whether brought about through this outward senseless nature, or by the will of man, good or bad, is overruled to each of us by the all-holy and all-loving will of God. Whatever befalls us, however it befalls us, we must receive as the will of God. If it befalls us through man's negligence, or ill-will, or anger, still it is, in even the least circumstance, to us the will of God. For if the least thing could happen to us without God's permission, it would be something out of God's control. God's providence or His love would not be what they are. Almighty God Himself would not be the same God; not the God whom we believe, adore, and love.[2]

The response (1:10)

Both Orpah and Ruth answer Naomi by saying that they will go back with their mother-in-law to her people in Judah. Even though they are Moabite widows and their prospects in Israel would not be good, yet they are willing to go. And it is not merely willingness on their part, but an emphatic resolve. The young women's statement begins with a Hebrew particle (kiy) that is best translated here as 'indeed!'[3] The word order of their speech also accentuates their message. The usual sentence construction in Hebrew is verb-subject-object. The young women's reply in this verse places the object first in the order of the sentence for emphasis; it literally reads, 'Indeed, with you we will return!' This last point underscores the reason that the women would go to Israel with Naomi, which is because of their loyalty to her. It is not for food or safety, or for any other reason; it is because they truly love their mother-in-law.

Naomi pushes back (1:11)

Naomi will not take 'no' for an answer. She is insistent. She tells the two of them to 'Turn back', or 'Return'. This verb is an imperative, and it is the same form as in verse 8. This repetition is emphatic. Although Naomi is forceful, however, she is not cruel. She calls Orpah and Ruth by the affectionate name 'my daughters'. This is the language of the family and is a term which reflects close kinship. What a wonderful, sweet comment for a mother-in-law to use to define her relationship with her daughters-in-law! What is driving Naomi to be so determined is her love and care for them.

Naomi then presents a logical argument. It is in the form of a rhetorical question: why in the world would they leave the comfort and advantages of home to follow her to a foreign land where they would be outsiders? Naomi has nothing to offer them. She is an aged widow with no sons and few prospects. She has no sons who could marry Orpah and Ruth. She has no sons in her womb; even if she did, would the young women wait until those sons grew to manhood?

In this verse we are being briefly introduced for the first time in the book to the important Hebrew cultural custom called 'the levirate law'. This law is succinctly summarized in Deuteronomy 25:5-6:

> If brothers dwell together, and one of them dies and has no son, the wife of the dead man shall not be married

39

outside the family to a stranger. Her husband's brother shall go in to her and take her as his wife and perform the duty of a husband's brother to her. And the first son whom she bears shall succeed to the name of his dead brother, that his name may not be blotted out of Israel.

The term 'levirate' derives from the Latin *levir,* which means 'husband's brother'. The Torah simply states that when a man dies and leaves a widow without male children, then the man's brother (the *levir*) shall marry her and have children in the dead brother's name. Although unfamiliar to us today, this custom was quite merciful and utilitarian: the widow was cared for; the inheritance remained within the clan structure, and the dead man's line was preserved. The levirate law will play an important role later in the book of Ruth. For now, Naomi is bluntly declaring that she has no son to perform this custom for Orpah and Ruth.

Return! (1:12-13)

Again Naomi demands that the young women leave her and stay in Moab. In verse 12, she begins with a double imperative: 'Return! ... Go!' These are the same volitional verb forms she used earlier, in verse 8; there, however, the order of the imperatives was reversed: 'Go! Return!' The alternation of the two imperatives is an example of what grammarians call a *chiasmus.* This is a common Hebrew technique to demonstrate emphasis — here it heightens the demand made by Naomi.

Naomi then presents another reason why the young women ought not to follow her. She is too old to have a husband and, therefore, she will remain a widow, suffering hardship and in difficulty, for the rest of her life. Then Naomi gives a 'what if' proposal: even if, miraculously, she might procure a husband that very night and then bear sons, would Orpah and Ruth wait until they were fully grown? This hypothetical scenario is, of course, absurd! Naomi is simply too old and she has no prospects! She then builds her argument by asking another rhetorical question: would these two young women really refrain from marriage and seclude themselves until the boys were grown? Consequently, Naomi is trying to impress on the women the hardship and trials that await them if they follow their mother-in-law.

In the middle of verse 13, Naomi is further insistent and resolute as she employs a strong Hebrew negative: *'No, my daughters...'* Her heart is vexed and full of bitterness. But why? In reality, her bitter spirit at this point is not because of her own harsh circumstances, but, rather, she tells the women it is *'for your sake'*, or 'on your account'. Naomi has a bitter taste in her mouth regarding the way that the adversity is affecting them. The natural reaction would obviously be for Naomi to regret and to be sorrowful over her own condition. But that is not the case: she is in despair because of Orpah and Ruth.

Naomi recognizes and acknowledges the sovereignty of God in her suffering. She states, *'The hand of the Lord has gone out against me.'* She clearly understands that, no matter what happens to her, whether it be good or ill, it is playing out according to the providence of God. Many people view adversity as a result of chance or circumstances; Naomi sees it as coming from the Lord's hand. She is correct. I wrote elsewhere:

> We are called to gauge our own hearts when we are in the slough of despond. We need to inquire of God and struggle with our situation in order to see why he is dealing with us in this particular way. And, for Christians,

41

we must remember that God is loving and caring toward his people, and he brings all things on them for their good and benefit. A friend of mine, stricken with cancer, once said to me, 'God brought this upon me, he entrusted this to me, because he knew I needed it, that it would be for my own good.'[4]

This is the second time Naomi mentions the covenantal name of Yahweh ('the Lord'). In verse 8, she calls for Yahweh to 'deal kindly' with Orpah and Ruth, and in the present verse she says that Yahweh deals harshly with her. At times, he stretches out his hand to his people, and at other times he pulls his hand away.

The great cling (1:14)

The response of the three women is the same as at the end of verse 9: 'they lifted up their voices and wept'. The emotional bond between the women is so strong; as Shakespeare once said, 'Parting is such sweet sorrow.' This latter phrase is an oxymoron, combining the ideas of sweet love and sorrowful parting. It accurately depicts the mood of the moment in this passage.

Then the text notes the first divergence of response between the two daughters-in-law. Orpah kisses her mother-in-law, but Ruth clings to her. The Hebrew verb 'to cling' is one that is used metaphorically as well as physically. It can express a state of loyalty, affection and intimacy. So, in Genesis 2:24, the verb is used to reflect the great intimacy that exists in marriage: 'Therefore a man shall leave his father and his mother and hold fast [literally, "cling"] to his wife, and they shall become one flesh.' Orpah's action is a goodbye kiss; she is dissuaded from going to Israel with Naomi. Ruth, on the other hand, will not be shaken or discouraged; she clings.

42

Points to ponder

1. God directs adversity

The idea that God allows, even directs, adversity to come on his own people is certainly a sound, biblical truth. *The Westminster Confession of Faith* summarizes this doctrine in the following manner:

> The most wise, righteous, and gracious God doth oftentimes leave, for a season, His own children to manifold temptations, and the corruption of their own hearts, to chastise them for their former sins, or to discover unto them the hidden strength of corruption and deceitfulness of their hearts, that they may be humbled; and to raise them to a more close and constant dependence for their support upon Himself, and to make them watchful against all future occasions of sin and for sundry other just and holy ends.[5]

One of the primary reasons that God brings adversity on Christians is so that they do not cling to the world. How often we rebel against the Lord, refusing to trust and rely upon him! We simply try to be self-reliant and look to the wisdom of the world. We put our 'trust in princes ... in whom there is no salvation' (Ps. 146:3). God, however, in his unfathomable grace, has, in the words of John Calvin, 'an excellent means to call us back, and to arouse us from our sluggishness, that our heart may not be too much attached to such foolish inclinations'. In short, God brings his people under the hand of affliction.

By means of adversity, God then restores believers to the dependence upon himself that is proper to creatures. That is to say that God frequently afflicts Christians so that they would

43

again realize that their hope, joy and sufficiency lie in him alone. God is thus being gracious in adversity, and uprooting the Christian from the world.

2. Humility or hubris?

The humility of Naomi in the midst of her extreme suffering is a worthy example of how believers ought to act in similar circumstances. She is not proud, and she places others before herself. There really is no room for hubris in the Christian life and walk. Unfortunately, I fear that many in the church today have a belief in their own self-sufficiency. Many have a lingering pride in who they are, and about what they can accomplish — this, of course, has led to such consequences as the cult of personality in the twenty-first-century evangelical church.

The reality is something different. The blessings of God do not come to his people through human strength or skill or craftiness or effort. They only come through the gracious provision of God to an undeserving people. The truth is that we do not need self-sufficiency; what we need is self-denial. We need to learn to be humble and meek, and to rely on the power of God to work in us and through us. Only Christ is all-powerful and all-sufficient. We ought to live out the words of Charles Spurgeon: 'If Christ be anything, he must be everything!'

Chapter 4
Ruth's confession

Please read Ruth 1: 15-18

Thomas Scott, an English preacher of the eighteenth century, is probably best known for his mammoth commentary on the whole Bible. The commentary is evangelical, Calvinistic, judicious and well-written. What is of great interest to us, however, is how Thomas Scott came to see and grasp the doctrines of grace.

In the 1770s, Scott was curate-in-charge of the parishes of Ravenstone and Weston Underwood in the Church of England. However, he was obviously an unbeliever: he denied the Trinity; he ridiculed the belief that the event at Calvary was a substitution and covering for sin, and he did not believe in hell, original sin or judgement. He did not believe that a person needed to be born again or regenerated by the Holy Spirit. Scott was also an uncaring pastor; he had very little to do with the people of his congregation. In fact, he had become a minister in order to have an easy way of making a living!

One day Scott began to hear rumblings in his parish that there was a Dissenter in the nearby town of Olney who was preaching strange things. So he slipped into the man's church to hear him preach. He couldn't believe the things he heard! And then he found out that this Dissenter had, in fact, visited two of Scott's parishioners who were on their deathbeds in order to encourage them in their trials. What audacity! Who did this man think he was, visiting members of Scott's congregation?

Scott did not like this Dissenting preacher. However, he began a written correspondence with the man in order to test his own theology. The Dissenter, John Newton, refused to argue with Scott. He simply laid out the gospel to him, prayed for him and assured him that one day he would come to agree with what Newton believed. Slowly Scott's mind and heart were changing. Brian Edwards comments:

> ... but not only his mind, his preaching also. To his great confusion, some of his congregation came to him 'in great distress about their souls', but he could only encourage them 'in a general way to believe in the Lord Jesus Christ'. Clearly some were converted before their own minister was!

In 1777, when he was going through a time of great trial and distress, Thomas Scott knew of only one man that he could turn to. John Newton helped him through the personal adversity. By the end of the trial, Scott became converted, evangelical and thereafter a Calvinist in his theology. Ironically, when Newton left Olney to pastor in London, it was Thomas Scott who 'took his place in the vicarage and wrote and preached as a champion for the truth', as Edwards notes.

One of the young men who often used to come and hear Scott preach was a young Baptist cobbler named William Carey. Carey commented in 1821: 'If there be anything of the word of God in my soul, I owe much of it to Scott's preaching.' Carey himself is known as the father of modern missions.

46

Oh, the mysterious providence of God in the salvation of sinners! We are about to witness such a sovereign event in the book of Ruth.

Go back! (1:15)

Orpah has left and returned to her people, her land and 'her gods'. Her decision, then, is not merely about social or economic issues — about how she will eat, live or find a husband — but it is a conscious spiritual decision. Orpah is returning to her gods, namely to the paganism and polytheism of the Moabites. The main god of Moab was Chemosh, and it appears that human sacrifice was part of the ritual associated with his worship (2 Kings 3:27). Orpah is simply not willing to relinquish her people, her home, her burial place, or her national gods.

And now, for a fourth time (see 1:8,11,12), Naomi employs the imperatival form 'return', or 'Turn back!', to urge Ruth to reconsider and go back with Orpah. One certainly cannot accuse Naomi of not being determined, or of not giving Ruth every opportunity to leave!

Ruth's commitment (1:16)

Ruth answers Naomi in a direct and strong way: 'Do not urge me...' That verb conveys gravity in Hebrew, and it is used ironically later in the book regarding the possibility of men 'assaulting' Ruth in the fields (2:22). Ruth is as resolute as Naomi, and tells her to stop the verbal assault on her. She does not want to follow Orpah; she is dedicated to Naomi and wants to follow at her heels.

47

What kind of commitment does Ruth have to Naomi? To what extent does her loyalty go? Ruth's proclamation to Naomi in this verse includes four examples of the construction known as idem per idem. This is a literary device in which the same verb or noun is used first of one person's actions and then of another person's actions. So, for example, Ruth says to Naomi, 'Where you go, I will go.' This literary technique is used to underscore the intensity of the action, as well as the totality of the commitment.

The first *idem per idem* is: '*Where you go I will go.*' Even if Naomi is to return to Israel, Ruth will not abandon her. She will cling to her mother-in-law despite the real possibility of danger and harm to herself. As I have repeatedly pointed out, Moab and Israel were long-standing enemies and were at odds with one another during the period of the judges, and thus the peril is substantial and present.

The second *idem per idem* construction is: '*Where you lodge I will lodge.*' This expression covers all circumstances in which she might be living. If Naomi's home is a hovel, Ruth will live with her; if it is a palace, Ruth will still live with her. The Spanish expression '*Mi casa, su casa*' summarizes Ruth's attitude well. And, indeed, Naomi's prospects in this regard are not good — what living arrangements will she face when she returns to Judah?

The next *idem per idem* is curt and to the point. In the original Hebrew it consists of a mere two words in which each possessive is part of a noun: 'Your people, my people.' Ruth is here denying her own Moabite people. She is laying aside her ancestral traditions, her home, her customs, her language and her blood relations. Instead, she will now embrace all of these things from an Israelite context and perspective.

The last in the line of these emphatic constructions in this verse is a blockbuster; it appears near the end, as a type of crescendo, or culmination, of Ruth's confession. It also consists of two words in Hebrew, which translate into English literally as, 'Your God, my God.' Back in verse 15 Orpah had returned to 'her gods' — that is, to the pagan deities of Moab. Ruth, on the other hand, renounces the gods of the Moabites and is now a willing follower of the Lord. Here she declares fidelity and allegiance to the God of Israel, and this represents a major shift from polytheism to monotheism.

Commitment unto death (1:17)

Ruth's loyalty to Naomi extends to the point of death. But it goes even beyond that. One would, of course, expect Naomi to die sooner than Ruth, and Ruth is saying that she will even be buried where Naomi is buried. Ruth is flatly stating that she will never return to Moab, but that she will be buried in Israel alongside Naomi. Her commitment is not only unto death, but unto the grave!

Ruth then takes a solemn oath that seals all the promises she has just made. And, most importantly, she invokes the name of Yahweh ('the Lord') to drive home the weight of her oath. This is the Hebrew covenantal, sacred name of God. She is not calling on the gods of Moab, but on the God of Israel. And she calls for Yahweh's judgement to come upon her if she is not faithful to her word; this oath is serious, sobering and binding. It is a malediction that petitions Yahweh's wrath to fall upon her if she breaks her promises in any way. Ruth then really drives home the oath by adding the words, 'and more also'; this is a call for even greater wrath to come upon her if she dares to break her bond and pledge.

49

Ruth's loyalty and commitment to Naomi are impressive. However, we do not want to miss the reality that Ruth appears to have become a resolute convert to the God of Israel. She has turned from paganism to the one true God. She has an unswerving loyalty and commitment to Yahweh as well as to Naomi.

A pregnant pause (1:18)

Ruth's conversion and solemn oath silence Naomi. Her mother-in-law has nothing more to say. She has been determined in telling Ruth to stay in Moab; Ruth, however, has been equally, if not more so, resolute in her desire to go with Naomi.

Points to ponder

1. Mysterious providence

The conversion of Ruth is a glorious event, but certainly one that is unexpected. She is a Moabite, and one steeped in the paganism of her society. But God is not thwarted or blocked by such things — oh, the mysterious providence of God in the salvation of sinners!

In the eighteenth century, the godly curate of St Giles Church in Reading, a Mr Talbot, died. He was to be replaced by a godless man, W. B. Cadogan, who had been educated at Oxford and had obtained many literary honours. According to John Newton:

> Mr Cadogan's views of religion were entirely different from those of his predecessor; and the people heard of his appointment with grief... Many left the church. Mrs

50

Talbot, however, considered it her duty to remain, hoping for a better state of things, and that she might encourage and help forward those to whom her husband's labours had been blessed. She opened her house for religious services, and invited clergymen like-minded with herself to conduct them. At the same time prayer was continually offered up under her roof for Mr Cadogan's conversion. By all this he was greatly offended. Letters passed full of remonstrance and even reproach on Mr Cadogan's part, but which Mrs Talbot's letters answered with meekness and wisdom. Mr Cadogan was overcome, and ever afterwards confessed that Mrs Talbot's letters and example were the principal means of leading him to the saving knowledge of Christ.

After that he preached the truths of Jesus, those truths that he had so strenuously opposed. Multitudes began to flock to hear him preach the gospel. As God had used Naomi to share the truth and be an example to Ruth, so Mrs Talbot did the same.

2. Genealogy

While the conversion of Ruth is an astounding event, we should, however, not forget the larger picture of God's redemptive history reflected in this story. In the genealogy of Jesus recorded by Matthew we read the following:

> The book of the genealogy of Jesus Christ, the son of David, the son of Abraham. Abraham was the father of Isaac, and Isaac the father of Jacob ... and Salmon the father of Boaz by Rahab, and Boaz the father of Obed by Ruth, and Obed the father of Jesse, and Jesse the father of David the king (Matt. 1:1-6).

The Jews of Jesus' day kept extensive genealogical records to establish a person's lineage, heritage and legitimacy. Matthew is writing his Gospel for a Jewish audience, and so he begins with Jesus' legal right and claim to the throne of David. Oddly, Jesus' genealogy includes four women. This is unusual because descent is normally traced through men only. In addition, two of the women, Rahab and Ruth, are Gentiles. This points to the truth of Gentile inclusion in the kingdom of God, and that Jesus has come to be Saviour of all sorts of people. As the apostle Paul teaches, 'There is neither Jew nor Greek, there is neither slave nor free, there is neither male nor female, for you are all one in Christ Jesus' (Gal. 3:28).

Chapter 5
Homecoming

Please read Ruth 1: 19-22

In the closing verses of Ruth chapter 1, Naomi clearly recognizes that her suffering and hardship ultimately come from the hand of God. Other scriptures confirm her view of the way the universe operates. For example, in the book of Ecclesiastes Solomon says, 'In the day of prosperity be joyful, and in the day of adversity consider: God has made the one as well as the other, so that man may not find out anything that will be after him' (Eccles. 7:14).

B. B. Warfield goes to the heart of the matter when he says, 'All things without exception, indeed are disposed by Him ... and if calamity falls upon man it is the Lord that has done it.'[1] Thus there are sweet providences and bitter providences in life, and Naomi acknowledges the reality of both in her own experience. All things derive from the Lord's hands, as the *Westminster Confession of Faith* proclaims:

> God, the great Creator of all things, doth uphold, direct, dispose, and govern all creatures, actions, and things, from the greatest even to the least, by His most wise and holy providence, according to His infallible foreknowledge, and the free and immutable counsel of His own will,

to the praise of the glory of His wisdom, power, justice, goodness, and mercy.[2]

The covenanter Alan Cameron understood this truth well.

[He was] the father of the well-known preacher Richard Cameron (the son was known by the epithet 'Lion of the Covenant'). For his covenanter views, Alan Cameron was placed in prison. One day the guards threw a sack into his cell; it contained a severed head and hands. The guards taunted the prisoner, 'Do you know them?' Cameron kissed the head, and he said, 'I know them. I know them. They are my son's, my own dear son's. It is the Lord. Good is the will of the Lord, who cannot wrong me or mine, but has made goodness and mercy to follow us all our days.'[3]

Bethlehem astir (1:19)

Naomi and Ruth leave Moab, travel together and both arrive in Bethlehem. When the two women enter the city the entire town responds, and it *'was stirred because of them'*. The Hebrew verb used here bears the idea of being in a commotion. The stem of the verb is passive/reflexive, and that means the people are experiencing inner turmoil; they are bewildered and confused.

The issue bringing commotion to the townspeople is *'them'* — that is, Naomi and Ruth. Two women come to town and they have no male escorts. One of them is old and the other is young. One is a Hebrew, the other a Moabite. What is their story? Why are they here? The whole town is in a twitter. Yet it appears that it is the women of Bethlehem who are particularly buzzing, and they ask, *'Is this Naomi?'* Who is this woman? Where is her family? Why is she travelling with a Moabite? It is not clear from the text whether the women are merely being curious, or vicious and malicious. In any event, they speak directly to Naomi because she responds to their questioning in the next verse.

A change of name (1:20)

Naomi responds directly to the women's question. She tells them not to call her 'Naomi'. Back in chapter 1 we defined the meaning of her name in Hebrew as 'sweet, pleasant, delightful' (see comments on 1:2); names, as we noted in that passage, often reflect a person's circumstances in life. Naomi does not want to be called 'sweet' any more because it does not reflect her life at this time. Rather, she employs an imperative saying, 'Call me Mara' instead. This word appears earlier in the book where Naomi says, 'It is exceedingly bitter to me for your sake that the hand of the Lord has gone out against me' (1:13). Thus, the people of Bethlehem are to call her 'bitter', and no longer call her 'sweet'. These antonyms echo Naomi's radically altered circumstances.

Naomi then describes the ultimate source of her bitter circumstances. She says it is because 'the Almighty has dealt very bitterly with me'. The verb 'to deal bitterly' is a cognate of the noun 'bitter', or 'Mara', by which Naomi now wants to be known. For the first time, Naomi refers to the Lord as 'the Almighty'; this name in Hebrew is Shaddai, and it is part of the name the patriarchs used for the God of the Hebrews (see, e.g., Gen. 17:1). Although often translated as 'almighty', the Hebrew word has more to do with the idea of God as the one who gives blessings to his people.[4] Consequently, Naomi is proclaiming that the God of blessings has withheld blessing from her, and instead has given her bitterness! We are again reminded that

55

sweet providences and bitter providences both proceed from the hand of God.

Yahweh deals with Naomi (1:20-21)

In these two verses, Naomi declares that the Lord has done four things to her:

A   *Shaddai* has dealt very bitterly with me
B   *Yahweh* has brought me back empty
B¹   *Yahweh* has testified[5] against me
A¹   *Shaddai* has brought calamity upon me

This structure is called a *chiasmus*, and its purpose is emphatic in order to demonstrate the fullness of God's activity coming against Naomi. She is truly *'empty'* at this point.

Is this wavering faith on Naomi's part? I don't believe so. On the contrary, it appears to be her recognition of God's providence in her life, albeit a bitter providence. She is, in fact, acknowledging God's hand in all the eventualities of life. And she then responds with endurance and perseverance. This is not wavering in faith, but facing difficult matters in faith.

> The Christian is called to run the race of life with endurance and fortitude. Flavel said, 'The upright soul abhors to flinch from his duty, let come on him what will.' Scripture encourages us to 'run with endurance the race that is set before us' (Heb. 12:1). The course may be long, treacherous, and uphill, but that does not matter. For we do not run the race in our own power, but 'I can do all things through him who strengthens me' (Phil. 4:13).[6]

56

A summary statement (1:22)

The biblical author summarizes the first chapter of the book by saying that Naomi and Ruth return from Moab and arrive in Bethlehem. No information is provided regarding the journey; they simply arrive safely in Judah.

One phrase is added to the summary that is worth noting. The text says that they come to Bethlehem 'at the beginning of barley harvest'. At first, this remark seems to be a mere temporal add-on — that is, it simply appears to be an aside that indicates the time of year when they arrive in Judah. Yet it is much more than an addendum indicating the time — God's timing needs to be seen in this statement. The barley harvest is the first harvest of grain during the agricultural year, and it has a short growing season. It is followed in a few weeks by the wheat harvest (see 2:23). These harvests are ones that will be rich in produce (see 1:6). Thus, Naomi and Ruth are arriving in Bethlehem at a time of plenty; they will not be without food. Naomi had left Judah because of lack of food; now she returns at a time of abundance! From famine (1:1) ... to plenty (1:22) — this is an *inclusio* that brackets the entire chapter.

In addition, a rich barley crop requires large numbers of workers in the field. God's timing is perfect. In God's providence, Ruth will find work in the fields and there meet Boaz. Therefore, this seemingly insignificant aside relating to the timing is, in reality, very important for the flow and purpose of the story. The barley crop is a sweet providence.

Points to ponder

1. The truly significant

The seemingly insignificant often plays a crucial role in God's providence. Consider a man such as Isaac Milner, who was, for the most part, an unknown tutor at Queen's College in Cambridge University. This man, though little known, laboured diligently and faithfully for Christ. He led William Wilberforce to Christ. Wilberforce, of course, later became an influential British politician, and he had a leading role in ending the slave trade in Britain. Milner also had a great impact on Charles Simeon when the latter was a student. Simeon went on to serve Christ faithfully in Trinity Church, Cambridge, for over fifty years, and many people came to Christ through his ministry. But who has ever heard of Isaac Milner? Yet this seemingly insignificant and minor figure greatly influenced Britain for Christ.

Recently I visited the site of Philippi in the region of Macedonia in north-eastern Greece. Two major historical events took place at this site.

First, a major battle took place here in 42 bc between the forces of Marc Antony and Octavius, on the one hand, and the troops of Cassius and Brutus, on the other. Cassius, dismayed at the apparent outcome of the battle, committed suicide; what he didn't know was that his troops had, in fact, won the battle. A few years later, Brutus also committed suicide as his army was destroyed by the forces of Octavius at Actium. With that victory, Octavius claimed undisputed supremacy over, and absolute power in, Rome.

The second event at Philippi was the visit of Paul, Timothy and Silas on the second missionary journey. Here, next to the river of the city, a noted conversion took place, that of Lydia. The first conversions in Europe occurred at Philippi.

It is interesting to compare these two events. At the time, certainly the second one seemed so insignificant, whereas the first one looked as though it would change the world. But what was the reality? Where is the Roman Empire today? On the other hand, the message that Paul and his companions brought to Europe was absolutely staggering in its impact and it continues to resound today.

2. Humility

God has humbled Naomi. He does this to his people. And what is the Lord's object in doing this? A. W. Pink comments:

> To bring us to the end of our own resources, to make us conscious of our own insufficiency, by bringing us into a situation from which we cannot extricate ourselves, confronting us with some obstacle which to human wit and might is insurmountable? By nature we are proud and self-reliant, ignorant of the fact that the arm of flesh is frail. And even faced with difficulties, we seek to solve them by our own wisdom, or get out of a tight corner by our own efforts. But the Lord is graciously resolved to humble us, and therefore the difficulties are increased and the corner becomes tighter, and for a season we are left to ourselves... It is not until we have duly weighed the difficulty and then discovered we have nothing of our own to place in the opposite scale, that we are really brought to realize our impotency, and turn unto him who alone can undertake for us and free us from our dilemma.[7]

Part 3:
In the fields of Bethlehem (2: 1-23)

Chapter 6
Ruth gleans in the fields

Please read Ruth 2: 1-7

The text to which we now come relates that Ruth just *'happened to come to the part of the field belonging to Boaz'* (2:2). A literal rendering of this passage is, 'it happened by chance' that she came into a portion of the field owned by Boaz. This is an ironic statement because we know that it did not occur by chance at all but, rather, by the sovereign plan of God himself. As Calvin remarks:

> Hence we maintain that by his providence, not heaven and earth and inanimate creatures only, but also the counsels and wills of men are so governed as to move exactly in the course he has destined. What, then, you will say, does nothing happen fortuitously, nothing contingently? I answer, it was a true saying of Basil the Great, that fortune and chance are heathen terms, the meaning of which ought not to occupy pious minds. For if all success is blessing from God, and calamity and adversity are his curse, there is no place left in human affairs for fortune and chance.[1]

The story which underpins the book of Ruth is the unfolding of the plan of God in history; there is no chance involved in it.

A parenthesis (2:1)

The author now shifts gears and introduces the reader to a new character who is central to the story. Boaz is 'a relative' of Naomi's husband. In the original Hebrew this word is a general one meaning 'an acquaintance'; Boaz is known to Elimelech, but the exact relationship between the two of them is not provided at this point. The ambiguity of this term certainly heightens the tension of the story and encourages the reader to ask, how close is Boaz really to Elimelech?

Boaz is a man of sterling character. The ESV says that he is 'a worthy man'. The Hebrew word used here is not the usual one for 'man', but rather it is a term meaning a 'mighty one'; the author employs the word to underscore Boaz's manliness. The word for 'worthy' can denote wealth in Hebrew, but it is also often used in a moral sense to refer to 'integrity, valour, and uprightness'. Interestingly, the same word is used later in the book to refer to Ruth's character (see 3:11). Boaz is simply a manly individual who is of high and trustworthy character.

Boaz's personal qualities are confirmed by the meaning of his name: 'In him is strength.' At a later point in time, when Solomon erects the temple in Jerusalem, we read the following account: 'He set up the pillars at the vestibule of the temple. He set up the pillar on the south and called its name Jachin, and he set up the pillar on the north and called its name Boaz' (1 Kings 7:21). These were the two main pillars of the temple complex, and they were sturdy and strong to hold up the temple. The point of the parallel is to underscore the strength of character of Boaz in the story of Ruth, and the fact that he is in a sense one of the pillars of the Israelite community in Bethlehem.

Finally, Boaz belongs to the 'clan' of Elimelech. A clan is an extended family structure that is multi-generational and

64

complex. It is based on the principle of consanguinity, which is that of blood relationship. Thus, we know now that Boaz is somehow related to Elimelech, but we are not yet certain how closely related he might be. The definition of the nature of that kinship will come later in the story.

Back to Naomi and Ruth (2:2)

Ruth shows deference to her mother-in-law by seeking her permission to go into the fields of Bethlehem to work. The biblical setting of Ruth's request is important to consider and understand. According to Israelite law, the Hebrew farmer was not to strip his fields bare. Leviticus 19:9-10 commands him:

> When you reap the harvest of your land, you shall not reap your field right up to its edge, neither shall you gather the gleanings after your harvest. And you shall not strip your vineyard bare, neither shall you gather the fallen grapes of your vineyard. You shall leave them for the poor and for the sojourner: I am the Lord your God.

This passage is part of a series of laws in the Torah dealing with the plight of the poor and the sojourner, and how a farmer is to respond to them (see Exod. 23:11; Lev. 23:22; Deut. 24:19-22). In this instance the agriculturalist is to leave the edges of his field unharvested, and he is to glean his field only once. The crops that are unharvested or missed are to be left for the disadvantaged in Israel. Such laws are gracious and merciful; they are wonderful provisions for the downcast and the outcast.

Ruth asks Naomi if she can go into the fields that are in the process of being harvested for barley (see 1:22). There she will follow the reapers and she will glean what has been missed. Ruth's request reflects some of her more important personality

65

traits: she is *industrious* and not afraid of hard work; she is *humble* and willing to perform menial labour in order to provide for Naomi and herself; she is *respectful* as she seeks her mother-in-law's approval to work in the fields.

In her request to Naomi, Ruth makes the vague statement that she will glean *'after him in whose sight I shall find favour'.* This general assertion simply means that Ruth doesn't yet know who will grant her gleaning rights. She is a Moabite and cannot assume such a privilege; apparently it is up to the owner of the field to extend the privilege, or right, to her. Although Ruth doesn't know who the owner might be, the reader already has a clue — the *'him'* will be Boaz, who has just been introduced in verse I of the chapter.

A chance encounter? (2:3)

With Naomi's blessing, Ruth goes to the fields to glean. She follows the reapers as they do their work, and she picks up the leftovers. The text, then, literally says, 'it happened by chance' that she comes to the portion of the field belonging to Boaz. How is the reader to understand this comment? Is it merely by luck, or chance, that she enters Boaz's field? The wording almost seems to deny the sovereignty of God that has been so evident in the book thus far — a theme which, I would argue, is primary throughout the entire book. How is the reader to deal with this statement?

The answer to this difficulty is to look at the situation from Ruth's perspective. She doesn't know that this field belongs to Boaz; she hasn't planned to work in this field. To her, it just happens. But, of course, the reader knows better. All is unfolding according to the mysterious providence of God — that is, it is

66

his plan that is coming to pass. Thus, the statement 'it happened by chance' reveals that Ruth is blind to the plan of God, but it is also an ironic or tongue-in-cheek remark by the author, who is well aware of God's providence at work.

The arrival of Boaz (2:4)

This verse begins with the emphatic particle 'behold'. In the Hebrew this is a word that tells the reader to give immediate attention to what is about to take place: 'Behold, Boaz!' The timing of Boaz's arrival is obviously perfect because God's timing is perfect. Here is the owner who just happened by chance (tongue-in-cheek) to come along to check on the work in his fields!

Boaz's appearance in the fields is worthy of our consideration. He is not an absentee landlord. He doesn't stay in his house and let others look after his holdings. No, he is *industrious* and unafraid of hard work. He is *humble*, as he doesn't think it is beneath him to work in the fields. And, as will be seen in the next verse, he is *respectful* of his workers in the field. Boaz's labours in the harvest are examples of why he is called 'a worthy man' in verse 1 of the present chapter.

The first words the reader hears out of Boaz's mouth are like a thunderclap. During these days of great apostasy, the time when the judges ruled (1:1), Boaz greets his workmen with *'The Lord* [Yahweh] *be with you!'* He uses the Hebrew covenantal name for God as he hails his field hands. The reapers respond with a literal, 'May Yahweh bless you!' In the original language the dialogue is constructed as a *chiasmus:*

a	b
Yahweh	be with you
a^1	b^1
May he bless you	Yahweh

This device underscores the completeness and emphasis of the greeting.

Boaz's question (2:5-7)

Boaz now turns discreetly to the chief reaper, and he asks about Ruth. He says, literally, 'To whom does this young woman belong?' Boaz is not asking specifically regarding the identity of Ruth's husband, but he is curious about her family tree. As one would say in the southern United States, 'Who are your people?' In Hebrew society all women were under some type of family authority, so whose care is this woman under?

The head of the reapers responds by simply saying, *'She is the young Moabite woman...'*, implying that Boaz would obviously know who he means. In other words, this is the woman that everyone in Bethlehem is talking about. She is the Moabitess who accompanied Naomi to Bethlehem. What she did has apparently given her a glowing reputation among the people of Judah; here is a pagan woman who has acted in an upright way. Thus we see that Ruth's reputation precedes her.

The chief reaper then further enhances Ruth's reputation. He tells Boaz that when the woman first came into the fields she asked for permission to glean during the harvest. She used the word *'please'*, which in the Hebrew language is a particle conveying deference. She was not demanding in any way; she was humble in her request. And, furthermore, the head reaper tells Boaz that Ruth showed up early in the morning and has worked steadily from then until Boaz's appearance.

The final clause of the chief reaper's words to Boaz is difficult to translate from the Hebrew. The ESV says that Ruth worked all day 'except for a short rest'. The text literally says, 'This is her dwelling; the house is little.' The word 'this' refers to the field, and it has been her residence all the day long. The 'house' in town has meant 'little' to her.[2] Therefore, this comment is an emphatic exclamation regarding Ruth's diligent and industrious character.

Ruth has certainly made quite an impression on Boaz's chief reaper, and for very good reason. She is diligent, caring, persevering and hard-working; she has integrity and fortitude. In fact, she is just like Boaz!

Points to ponder

1. A chance happening

As Ruth does her duty to help feed herself and Naomi, she 'happens by chance' to enter a field belonging to Boaz. Isn't that how life often works for God's people? We travel on our pilgrimage, and we bumble our way through things; we are ignorant of much that goes on around us — yet, when we look back over our lives, isn't it often in the most insignificant things that we see God's hand working? It is true what John Flavel once said: 'Some providences are like the letters of the Hebrew language; they must be read backwards.' And so we look back on our history and we 'know that for those who love God all things work together for good, for those who are called according to his purpose' (Rom. 8:28). And we see, perhaps as a glimpse, or in

69

a mirror dimly, that we are part of a grander plan, and that God uses what we deem insignificant in a mighty way for his purposes.

As I look back over my many years of preaching, it is enlightening to remember how often God used what I thought was a passing or insignificant comment to touch someone's heart with a biblical truth. And sometimes I don't even remember making the remark that the person later shares with me! How we are to be reminded that it is God's power and plan that are in operation, and not our own! The Scotsman Robert Burns writes in his poem 'To a Mouse, or Turning her up in her Nest with the Plough', the following:

> But little Mouse, you are not alone,
> In proving foresight may be vain:
> The best-laid schemes of mice and men
> Go often askew,
> And leave us nothing but grief and pain,
> For promised joy!

2. Virtue

The period of the judges was one of great moral decay in the land of Israel; it was a time when 'everyone did what was right in his own eyes' (Judg. 21:25). In that context, it is precious to see someone like Ruth, with such a character of integrity and virtue — and, most amazingly, she was a Moabite! She was, however, a believer, and one worth emulating. C. H. Spurgeon poignantly states, 'A good character is the best tombstone. Those who loved you, and were helped by you, will remember you. So carve your name on hearts, and not on marble.'

Our characters can be a wonderful testimony to the gospel and to the work of Christ in us. A contemporary account of John Bunyan's character, written at the time of his death, says:

> He appeared in countenance to be of a stern and rough temper, but in his conversation mild and affable; not given to loquacity or much discourse in company, unless some urgent occasion required it; observing never to boast of himself or his parts, but rather seen low in his own eyes, and submit himself to the judgement of others; abhorring lying and swearing, being just in all that lay in his power to his word, not seeming to revenge injuries, loving to reconcile differences and make friendship with all; he had a sharp quick eye, accomplished with an excellent discerning of persons, being of good judgement and quick wit. As for his person, he was tall of stature, strong-boned, though not corpulent, somewhat of a ruddy face, with sparkling eyes, wearing his hair on his upper lip, after the old British fashion; his hair reddish, but in his latter days time had sprinkled it with grey; his nose well set, but not declining or bending, and his mouth moderate large; his forehead something high, and his habit always plain and modest. And thus we have impartially described the internal and external parts of a person whose death hath been much regretted — a person who had tried the smiles and frowns of time, not puffed up in prosperity nor shaken in adversity, always holding the golden mean.
>
> In him at once did three great worthies shine:
> historian, poet, and a choice divine:
> then let him rest in undisturbed dust,
> until the resurrection of the just.

Chapter 7
Conversations between Ruth and Boaz

Please read Ruth 2: 8-17

In this passage (2:8-17) we are struck by the compassion and kindness that Boaz shows to Ruth. True compassion is a sign of a believer who is becoming more and more like the Lord. In Mark 1:40-45, we see the wonderful compassion of Jesus, and it is something that his people ought to imitate. A leper comes to him asking him, 'If you will, you can make me clean.' This is an amazing scene, especially in the light of our understanding of how people with skin diseases were viewed during the biblical period. According to Leviticus 13 – 14, this man is to be shunned and kept isolated outside the camp of Israel; he is to have no contact with fellow Hebrews, and he is certainly not to have contact with the religious rites of the temple. He could only resume religious practices if and when he was pronounced clean by the priesthood. He is to walk around with his hair unkempt, his clothes in tatters and his mouth covered. And when anyone is within hearing distance, he is to cry out the words: 'Unclean, unclean' (Lev. 13:45). He is not allowed to enter walled cities, and his only contact is to be with other lepers.

By New Testament times, the prohibitions regarding lepers were quite complex and detailed. In the Talmud, there is a section called the 'Code of Defilements', and in it is a ranking of things that make a person unclean. At the top of the list is leprosy, and it is called 'the father of uncleanness'. The rabbinic leaders of the day confess that they are powerless in the presence of this living death. In fact, they argue that it is easier to raise the dead than to cure a leper! The religious leaders of the day avoided lepers; they were not allowed to salute or even wave to them. There are contemporary accounts of leaders throwing stones at lepers and hiding themselves from these disease-ridden people.

In Mark 1, on the other hand, we see a rabbi who does not run away or throw stones at them. No, in verse 41 it says that he is 'moved with pity', or 'compassion'. Jesus is drawn by the man's broken condition. But we need to note that Jesus doesn't merely have a sense of pity for the man's plight; he acts upon it. He stretches out his hand and touches the leper! Jesus has such compassion that he heals the man using skin-to-skin contact. He himself becomes ritually infected and unclean in order to cleanse the leper. Such compassion is unique and astounding.

Boaz's compassion in the episode with Ruth reflects the compassion of Christ. Martin Luther once said, 'It is the duty of every Christian to be Christ to his neighbour.' Because Christ showed such mercy to us, we ought to have compassion on others.

Boaz's protection (2:8-9)

After receiving the report about Ruth from his foreman, Boaz now turns to speak directly to Ruth. This is exceptional in that the owner of the field speaks to one of the indigent sojourners who are gleaning behind his workers. And, what is more, he is especially kind to her, and he speaks to her in a tone of deference and respect. In his opening remarks to her, Boaz calls her 'my daughter' (2:8). This is a term of endearment and benevolence; it is how Naomi had addressed Ruth earlier in the book (see 1:11; 2:2). It may perhaps also indicate an age difference or generation gap between the two of them — something that Boaz in fact comments on later (see 3:10). The opening statement is actually in the form of a question in the original, saying literally, 'Will you not listen, my daughter?' This is a request, and not a demand. Again, Boaz is not acting the part of the overlord, but he is showing courtesy to the woman.

Boaz encourages Ruth not to glean in other fields, but to stay in his holdings. He does not tell her to stop gleaning — only that she should do it within the confines of his possession of land. He recognizes her industriousness and he reassures her in her labours. Boaz, however, also gives Ruth a stiff warning: 'but keep close to my young women'. That verb in Hebrew means to 'cling', or 'cleave' (see, e.g., Gen. 2:24, in which the ESV translates it as 'hold fast').

And why does Boaz make this offer? First, these 'young women' in a sense belong to him; Boaz uses the possessive 'my' with regard to them. The designation 'young women' is normally used of young, unmarried women, and not of servants or slaves. These are probably women of his clan. They are, therefore, well protected. Ruth will be safe and secure in Boaz's field and among the women of his family. Ruth is to glean with Boaz's gleaners, and not way back in the field along with the indigent. Perhaps another reason why Boaz elevates Ruth is so that she will find enough food for her family.

In verse 9, Boaz repeats his charge to Ruth that she needs to be focused on gleaning only in his field and to follow close upon his workers. And, then, he asks her a rhetorical question: 'Have I

75

not charged the young men not to touch you?' Obviously, Boaz has already given this order, and he did it in such a way that Ruth could overhear it. Through various means, Boaz is attempting to protect Ruth and to safeguard her well-being. The reality is that almost anything can happen to a person who is alone in a field with no authorities present (see, e.g., the story of Cain and Abel in Gen. 4:8).

Boaz not only protects Ruth, but he lavishly provides for her sustenance in the field where she works. She is free to partake of the water that is provided for the labourers in the field. Ruth need not bring her own water to work, nor does she have to draw her own. She may drink freely from what the male workers draw. Water was, of course, a highly valued commodity in the ancient Near East. One of the principal causes of famine is drought; Israel has just experienced an extended famine. Water is precious. And in this scene Boaz tells Ruth to drink of it to her heart's content.

Ruth's response (2:10)

Ruth reacts immediately to Boaz's kindness by falling on her face and bowing to the ground. These actions are a common way in the Old Testament of signifying humility in the presence of another. They also reflect the respect that one has for someone who is in a position of authority. Ruth then asks Boaz, *'Why have I found favour in your eyes?'* This is a question expressing astonishment and awe; she is wondering who she is and what she has done to be treated so well.

Ruth's amazement is accentuated as she observes that Boaz has taken notice of her even though she is a foreigner. In the original there is a play on words: the word *'foreigner'* is related to the verb translated as *'take notice'*. The latter verb in Hebrew literally

76

means 'to recognize' and the noun used for 'foreigner' literally means 'the unrecognizable one'. A foreigner in Israel receives no recognition, and so Ruth questions Boaz in wonder — why does he give her special recognition?

Boaz's answer (2:11-12)

Boaz responds to Ruth's question by describing what he has heard about her from others. Yes, he has heard from the foreman in the field, but from others as well. He says to her, it *'has been fully told to me'*. This construction in Hebrew is a double verb, and it is emphatic, indicating that Boaz has received a full report — perhaps more than one — regarding Ruth's behaviour towards her mother-in-law. The account of Ruth's actions has really made the rounds of the town. Boaz has thus received good reports from various quarters.

The respect Boaz has for Ruth is not only because of her treatment of Naomi, but also because she has left her family and country. She has done a courageous thing by leaving her home and her people to come to a land she does not know.

Boaz, in verse 12, pronounces a blessing on Ruth. He begins by saying, *'The Lord* [Yahweh] *repay you for what you have done'*. The word the ESV translates as *'repay'* is actually a verb from which the noun *'shalom'* derives. It basically signifies 'to bring something to completion, to bring peace, to bring about harmony'. Boaz is calling for Yahweh, the covenant God of Israel, to bring Ruth's deeds and conduct to full fruition and use them extensively. Secondly, he asks God to give Ruth *'a full reward'*; the word *'full'* is the feminine of the word *'shalom'*. In other words, Boaz is asking that God would give Ruth a complete, full *'reward'*; this latter noun normally signifies a person's wages.

Boaz's oath ends with '... *under whose wings you have come to take refuge!'* Boaz pictures Ruth as one who has sought the protection of Yahweh. The metaphor of the Lord as a mother bird who protects her young under her wings is a common one in the Old Testament and, in particular, regarding Israel's deliverance from the oppression in Egypt. For example, Deuteronomy 32:11-12 describes the Lord's care of Israel in the wilderness, as follows:

> Like an eagle that stirs up its nest,
>   that flutters over its young,
> spreading out its wings, catching them,
>   bearing them on its pinions,
> the Lord alone guided him,
>   no foreign god was with him.

And Exodus 19:4 tells how God brought Israel out of Egypt to Mount Sinai: 'You yourselves have seen what I did to the Egyptians, and how I bore you on eagles' wings and brought you to myself.' The language of these two passages reflects God's protection of his people as it depicts him in terms of a mother bird hovering over and guarding its young.

Ruth's reply (2:13)

Ruth has the final word in the opening conversation between her and Boaz. The ESV translates the first clause of her speech as '*I have found favour in your eyes.*' However, in the original it is not a declaration, but rather a request, or plea. It literally says, 'May I find favour in your eyes?' On the basis of what Boaz has already done for her, Ruth is anticipating further kindness from him. She is fully entrusting herself to his care, goodness and kindness.

She may also be encouraging Boaz. This would be reciprocal because she has received great encouragement from him. She says, 'for you have comforted me' — that is, he has consoled her and has eased her sorrow and pain.[1] Boaz, has also, literally, 'spoken to the heart of your maidservant'. The Hebrew word used for 'heart' is not merely the seat of emotion in a person, but it signifies the very core of one's being. It is the *persona*, the mind, the will, the desire, the emotion and the intention of the individual concerned. Boaz has thus spoken to the very depths of her being.

Ruth, finally, expresses her surprise that Boaz has dealt with her this way. She is a mere 'servant'. And, even more to the point, she is not one of Boaz's 'servants'. Here again the reader ought to be struck by Ruth's humility and honesty.

Another kindness (2:14)

Some time later in the day, Boaz, obviously noting that Ruth has no provisions, invites her to a meal with his work party. He gives her bread, wine and roasted grain. Boaz thus surpasses his earlier kindness by asking Ruth to participate in a meal that he provides for his workers.

Ruth takes a seat near Boaz's reapers. There is a certain acceptance reflected in this seating: she is not alone, nor is she ostracized or rejected because she is an indigent Moabitess. She is not being treated as an outsider or outcast. This seating arrangement also has a utilitarian purpose. Ruth is now protected from any dangers lurking in the fields.

Boaz gives her 'roasted grain'. This is grain that has been prepared elsewhere and then brought to the fields for a meal (cf. 1 Sam.

79

17:17; 25:18). He hands to Ruth an abundance of food — she eats, she is satisfied, and she even has some left over. We need to see that Boaz is not merely caring for Ruth, but he is lavishing things upon her.

Further protection and abundance (2:15-16)

Even with all of Boaz's charity to her, Ruth gets up from her meal to glean. She doesn't take advantage of his kindness. She knows that she must still provide sustenance for Naomi and herself, and so she is diligent. For his part, Boaz does not restrain her, but he gives orders to his workers concerning her: he literally says, 'Indeed, between the sheaves let her glean!'[2] This is another gracious act on the part of Boaz. According to Hebrew law, the poor could go after, or behind, the reapers and gleaners, and then pick up the remains that had not been harvested. Boaz is saying that Ruth can glean right in the areas where his young men are labouring. Thus she will not merely get the leftovers of the crop, but the very best pickings!

Boaz then orders his men not to 'reproach' her. This is a general term in Hebrew that can have a physical application (i.e., 'molest') and a verbal application (i.e., 'verbal abuse'). The reapers are not to humiliate or shame Ruth in any way. Human nature is such that people take advantage of those who are less fortunate. We tend to look down on others, and to oppress them easily. Boaz is not going to allow that to happen to Ruth.

But there is more! The opening words of verse 16 are 'And also...' An additional grace will be bestowed on Ruth. Boaz tells the workers to leave bundles of grain on the ground on purpose so that Ruth can easily pick them up and bind them. In Hebrew, this command is a double verb (an infinitive followed

80

by an imperfect of the same verb): it literally reads, 'pulling out, pull out...' This is a common Hebrew grammatical device for the purpose of emphasis. The workers are clearly to obey this command.

And, finally, Boaz orders the men, 'do not rebuke her'; the negative here is an apodictic 'no', which is the severest form of negative in the Hebrew language. The men are simply not to menace this woman.

Ruth gleans (2:17)

According to verse 7 of this chapter, Ruth came to the field and began gleaning in the early morning hours. She now ends her labours at evening; she has put in a full day's work in the fields. But she does more: she goes in the evening to 'beat out' what she had gleaned. Her activity is threshing — that is, she is separating the grain from the husks of what she had gleaned. Threshing normally takes place at a threshing floor, which is a large, flat slab of rock located in a windy place. The worker first drags some type of heavy sledge over the plant material which breaks it down into its constituent elements. Then the farmer winnows it, often using some type of large fork, and this separates the wheat from the chaff.

This is, of course, hard labour. Ruth reaps the reward of her hard work, however. She ends up, at the close of the day, with about an 'ephah' of barley. An 'ephah' is a measure of dry capacity that is equal to 3/8 to 2/3 bushel.[3] This amounts to approximately twenty pounds of barley, which is a generous amount of grain.

81

Points to ponder

1. The character of the characters

Are we not struck by the kindness, humility, compassion and diligence of both Ruth and Boaz? They both do their duty, but they do it with integrity and strong character. Elizabeth Elliot once wrote:

> What can I do for God? Most of us would like to do something special in life, something to distinguish us. We suppose that we desire it for God's sake, but more likely we are discontent with ordinary life and crave special privileges. When Israel asked if they should offer some spectacular sacrifice — thousands of rams, ten thousand 'rivers of oil,' a firstborn child — the answer was, 'He has showed you, O man, what is good; and what does the Lord require of you but to do justice, and to love kindness, and to walk humbly with your God?' (Mi 6:8 RSV). There is nothing conspicuous about those requirements. It is not a 'special' service for which one would be likely to be decorated or even particularly remembered. But it is worth more to God than any sacrifice.

2. Compassion on a foreigner

How we live and act is greatly influenced by any number of factors: our environment, our standing in society, our economic status, our religious beliefs, our heredity and, perhaps most of all, our family. Boaz's kindness to Ruth has some family history: Boaz's mother was Rahab, the Canaanite prostitute (Josh. 2:1-24). Rahab had been a pagan prostitute in the city of Jericho prior to Israel's conquest of that city. She had, however, been converted and she hid the Hebrew spies whom Joshua had sent to reconnoitre the city. The author to the Hebrews comments, 'By faith Rahab the prostitute did not perish with those who were disobedient, because she had given a friendly welcome to the spies' (Heb. 11:31).

Joshua 6:25 tells the reader that Rahab settled among the covenant people: 'And she has lived in Israel to this day, because she hid the messengers whom Joshua sent to spy out Jericho.' She married a man named Salmon (Ruth 4:20-21; 1 Chr. 2:11), and then gave birth to Boaz (Matt. 1:4-5; Luke 3:32). Thus we see that Boaz is, at least with regard to physical descent, half-Gentile and half-Israelite. No wonder he has such compassion on a pagan woman who has converted to the faith of the Hebrews! It is also striking that both women, Rahab and Ruth, are included in the genealogy of the Messiah, the Son of David (Matt. 1:5).

Chapter 8
Ruth reports to Naomi

Please read Ruth 2: 18-23

For the first time in the book of Ruth the reader is introduced to the title 'redeemer' (2:20). The Hebrew term is *goel*, and it literally refers to one who is a 'kinsman-redeemer'. The Hebrew verb from which this title derives means 'to avenge, redeem, ransom, and to do the part of a kinsman'.[1] Inherent in this word is the idea that a person would deliver a member of his family from difficult circumstances.

In ancient Israel, the kinsman-redeemer *(goel)* has four basic duties. First, he has the obligation to buy back his kin from bondage or slavery. If a Hebrew gets himself into debt, he could indenture himself to another Hebrew, or to a sojourner in the land, in order to pay off what he owes. The kinsman-redeemer needs to secure that person's release. Leviticus 25:47-49 states:

> If a stranger or sojourner with you becomes rich, and your brother beside him becomes poor and sells himself to the stranger or sojourner with you or to a member of the stranger's clan, then after he is sold he may be redeemed. One of his brothers may redeem him, or his uncle or his cousin may redeem him, or a close relative

from his clan may redeem him. Or if he grows rich he may redeem himself (see also Deut. 15:12-17).

Secondly, the *goel* has the duty to buy back land that one of his relatives had sold. Again, a Hebrew who goes into debt may sell his land to pay off what he owes. The kinsman-redeemer is required to redeem it. Leviticus 25:23-25 says:

> The land shall not be sold in perpetuity, for the land is mine. For you are strangers and sojourners with me. And in all the country you possess, you shall allow a redemption of the land. If your brother becomes poor and sells part of his property, then his nearest redeemer shall come and redeem what his brother has sold.

Thirdly, if a female is a widow in the clan and has no male heirs, then the *goel* has the responsibility to marry her. This levirate law is for the protection of the widow and to produce a succession to, and a progeny for, the dead husband. It also makes certain that the land inheritance stays within the clan. The reader should consult the comments on Ruth 1:11.

Finally, the kinsman-redeemer is to act as the avenger of blood on behalf of his relatives. In the law we read the following with regard to an act of murder:

> But if he struck him down with an iron object, so that he died, he is a murderer. The murderer shall be put to death. And if he struck him down with a stone tool that could cause death, and he died, he is a murderer. The murderer shall be put to death. Or if he struck him down with a wooden tool that could cause death, and he died, he is a murderer. The murderer shall be put to death. The avenger [Hebrew, *goel*] of blood shall himself put the

86

murderer to death; when he meets him, he shall put him to death (Num. 35:16-19).

The primary work of the kinsman-redeemer is redemption. And redemption bears as its central concept the faithfulness, obligations and duty of the next of kin. Blood is thicker than water, and family must care for relatives. Redemption, then, can be defined as 'a process by which something alienated might be restored by a kinsman-redeemer'. This concept will play a major role throughout the remainder of the book of Ruth.

Ruth returns home (2:18)

Ruth lifts up her 'ephah' of barley and she returns to the town of Bethlehem from the threshing floor. The ESV then says, *'Her mother-in-law saw what she had gleaned.'* Some early manuscripts[2] actually make Ruth the active one here by translating it as, 'and she showed to her mother-in-law what she had gleaned'. In addition, Ruth gives Naomi, literally, 'the leftover of her satisfaction'. To what does this refer? The same wording is found in Ruth 2:14, which reads, '... she was satisfied, and she had some left over.' Ruth is simply giving Naomi the leftover roasted grain that Boaz had given her at mealtime in the fields!

How thoughtful of Ruth! It certainly would have been a strain merely to bring home the barley, but she also brings a meal for Naomi. Ruth, as is her custom, places others before herself. Such action is a true sign of faith. The apostle Paul remarks in 1 Timothy 5:8, 'But if anyone does not provide for his relatives, and especially for members of his household, he has denied the faith and is worse than an unbeliever.'

Naomi's amazement (2:19)

Naomi is surprised by what she sees. Her astonishment is confirmed by her repetition of the question: *'Where did you glean today? And where have you worked?'* Obviously, Naomi is stunned by how much produce Ruth has brought back from the fields, and by the additional provision of the roasted grain. She is eager to hear Ruth's story. Naomi then invokes a blessing on her anonymous benefactor: *'Blessed be the man who took notice of you.'*[3] Naomi recognizes and acknowledges that some landowner has heaped great kindness on Ruth. She thus breaks forth in praise and exclamation.

Ruth responds with a detailed report of all that had transpired in the fields. She also provides the name of the man for whom she had worked — *'Boaz'*. His name is presented at the very end of the verse; it is a climactic pronouncement. This is dramatic suspense.[4] The reader has known who the man is right from the opening verse of the chapter, and Ruth has known by working in his field; Naomi is the one who is now let in on his identity.

Hallelujah! (2:20)

After hearing that the man is Boaz, Naomi breaks forth into great praise. For a second time, she calls for this man to be *'blessed'* (see 2:19). In the first blessing, the man was anonymous, but in the second he is well known. Naomi also adds to the second blessing by asking for it to come by Yahweh, the covenant God of Israel.

Naomi then says in her blessing, *'whose kindness has not forsaken the living or the dead!'* The term *'whose'* is ambiguous — does it refer to Yahweh or Boaz? A key is the use of the word *'kindness'*

(Hebrew *chesed*). It has already appeared in the book in chapter 1:8, where Naomi calls for Yahweh to deal 'kindly' with Ruth. By bringing Boaz into the picture, the Lord is dealing kindly with Ruth, *'the living'*, and perhaps Boaz will also serve as a kinsman-redeemer, and thus raise up seed for *'the dead'*.

The ambiguity may be deliberate, however. Boaz embodies a character of kindness (see 2:8-9,14-16). In that regard, he echoes God's own character. His generosity to Ruth goes way beyond the legal requirements of the law. He is gracious, as God is gracious.

Naomi does have some information of which Ruth is unaware. She gives this marvellous revelation: literally, 'The man is near to us.' This is an idiomatic expression in the Bible for one who is a close relative (see 2 Sam. 19:42). But how close a relation is he? Naomi defines the relationship a little more by saying, he is *'one of our redeemers'*. In Hebrew law, there is an order, or rank of obligation, among redeemers: 'One of his brothers may redeem him, or his uncle or his cousin may redeem him, or a close relative from his clan may redeem him' (Lev. 25:48-49).

The sequence of obligation to redeem in this text progresses from the closest relatives, the brothers, to the most distant blood relatives in the clan. The exact position of Boaz in the ranking is not yet revealed in the text. The drama of the story is moving forward at a high pitch.

Ruth relays further information (2:21-22)

Ruth tells Naomi about further conversation that she had with Boaz. She begins her speech with an emphatic particle that literally means 'Yes, indeed' (the ESV translates it as *'Besides'*).

89

With this introduction Ruth is trying to emphasize for Naomi the extraordinary kindness of Boaz to her.

Boaz had told Ruth in the field to 'cling' (see the discussion of this verb in the comments on 1:14) to the young women, literally, 'who belong to me', until they have finished all the harvest 'which belongs to me'. This repetitive expression underscores Boaz's position as the one in authority and the owner of the fields. Boaz is an important man in Bethlehem, a pillar of the community; could there really be a place for Ruth in his life? How could a Moabite widow ever expect such treatment as that which she has received from him?

Note also that Ruth is called a *'Moabite'* in this verse. She was called that at the beginning of the chapter too (2:2). This is what Hubbard calls an 'inclusio of identity', since it introduces Ruth's first and last words in the chapter.[5] The reader is thus reminded again and again of Ruth's lowly position and status in Israel.

Time marches on (2:22-23)

Naomi responds to Ruth's news by encouraging her to continue to glean in Boaz's fields with his young women. Naomi instructs Ruth to do so lest she be *'assaulted'* in someone else's field. That verb is a strong one in Hebrew referring to molestation, or falling prey to another person (see Josh. 2:16; Judg. 8:21; 15:12). Although it is unstated, it is likely that Naomi has already begun planning in her mind regarding the relationship between Boaz and Ruth. He is a man with good prospects!

Ruth once again obeys her mother-in-law. She works in Boaz's fields during both the barley and wheat harvests. This period of her labours in the fields amounts to approximately three

90

months. All this time she lives with, and provides for, Naomi and herself. She is faithful to Naomi, and she is keeping her pledge of Ruth 1:16: 'For where you go I will go, and where you lodge I will lodge.'

Points to ponder

The concept of redemption by a *goel*, to which the reader is introduced in the book of Ruth, is, in reality, a wonderful picture used in the Bible of God's work for his people. Throughout the Old Testament, the term *goel* is used of the Lord. Job, for example, proclaims:

> For I know that my Redeemer [= *goel*] lives,
> and at the last he will stand upon the earth.
> And after my skin has been thus destroyed,
> yet in my flesh I shall see God
> (Job 19:25-26).

David echoes Job by announcing:

> Let the words of my mouth and the meditation of my
> heart be acceptable in your sight,
> O Lord, my rock and my redeemer
> (Ps. 19:14).

The great redemptive event of the Old Testament is the exodus out of Egypt. In Exodus 5:22 – 6:8, the Lord tells Moses that he is acting as goel for his people. In Exodus 6:6 he announces that he is about to redeem Israel from bondage and slavery. He then claims that he will redeem the land of promise for his people (v. 8). He will act as the avenger of blood when he destroys the firstborn of Egypt. The Lord cares for his family by bringing

91

his people out of Egypt; he, in fact, refers to his people as his firstborn (Exod. 4:22-23).

In the New Testament, Jesus is portrayed as the goel of his people. We read in Luke 4:16-21:

> And he came to Nazareth, where he had been brought up. And as was his custom, he went to the synagogue on the Sabbath day, and he stood up to read. And the scroll of the prophet Isaiah was given to him. He unrolled the scroll and found the place where it was written,
>
> The Spirit of the Lord is upon me, because he has anointed
>   me to proclaim good news to the poor.
> He has sent me to proclaim liberty to the captives and
>   recovering of sight to the blind,
> to set at liberty those who are oppressed,
> to proclaim the year of the Lord's favour.
>
> ... And he began to say to them, 'Today this Scripture has been fulfilled in your hearing.'

Jesus here claims to be the one who will bring release and liberty to his people; he is the *goel* for the believer.

What a glorious picture! Jesus is the *goel* who has released his kin from bondage to sin (Rom. 3:21-25; Eph. 1:7). He has reclaimed an inheritance for his people (Heb. 9:15; 1 Peter 1:3-4). He has raised up a seed in his name (Eph. 1:5). And, finally, he is the blood avenger to those who have persecuted, mistreated and killed his people (see the book of Revelation). With the blood of Christ believers have been redeemed from their sin and from the wrath of God, and it is an eternal redemption. Jesus, the true kinsman-redeemer, has come!

Part 4:
The scene at the threshing floor (3: 1-18)

Chapter 9
Naomi's plan

Please read Ruth 3: 1-6

Genesis 38 presents the story of Judah and Tamar; it has some interesting ties to the book of Ruth.[1] The story generally unfolds as follows: Judah took a wife for his son Er, but that son soon died because of his wickedness. So Judah commands his next son, Onan, to perform the levirate law, and thus to raise seed in his dead brother's name. Onan, however, skirts the law and he dies because of his disobedience. Judah has a young son named Shelah, and he promises Tamar that Shelah will perform the levirate law when he grows up. However, after Shelah does grow up, Judah does not keep his word (v. 14). He does not fulfil his responsibility to Tamar in the matter of the levirate law.

Tamar does not remain passive, but she acts to force the issue. Apparently she has little recourse, yet through her actions she shames Judah into seeing that he has violated the law of the *levir*. Ironically, Tamar is impregnated by Judah, and she gives birth to two sons named Perez and Zerah. This story is later given prominence in the book of Ruth because Perez is an ancestor of David (4:12,18).

In one sense Naomi and Ruth are like Tamar because they appear to have little recourse, or leverage, in the matter of the levirate law. They have been back in Bethlehem for at least three months, but there has not been any movement or action on the part of a kinsman-redeemer. As a result of this inactivity, Naomi, in the early verses of chapter 3, decides to act and to help push along the redemptive process.

Naomi's concern for Ruth's welfare (3:1)

Naomi ponders Ruth's welfare. She is concerned that Ruth should find 'rest', peace and security (see Ps. 116:7). At this point in time Ruth, as a Moabite widow and sojourner, is still vulnerable. Certainly part of Naomi's motivation is her affection for her daughter-in-law; she obviously and clearly cares for Ruth. But Naomi is also certainly moved by other considerations. In particular, Elimelech's line is in jeopardy, and it needs to be preserved for reasons of inheritance and the continuation of his name. The preservation of Elimelech's line appears to be Naomi's overriding concern at this point.

When Naomi addresses Ruth she begins by saying, 'My daughter, should I not seek...?' This is a negative in the form of a question. However, in Hebrew this construction actually often expresses clear certainty in the sense of 'it is my duty to seek'. Thus, Naomi's dialogue here is not so much a question as a forceful statement: 'I will seek!' Naomi has a sense of urgency to find a husband for Ruth through the laws of redemption. She is afraid that Elimelech's inheritance might have to be sold and thus pass outside the family. A *goel* would preserve the inheritance, and then Naomi would be taken care of in her old age. Ruth would also be cared for.

In Ruth 1:9 Naomi had called for a blessing from the Lord to come upon both Orpah and Ruth. That blessing was that each daughter-in-law would find 'rest' in the house of a husband. Naomi is now playing an integral part in the fulfilment of that blessing for Ruth.

The plan unfolds (3:2)

Naomi now begins to reveal her plan to secure a kinsman-redeemer for Ruth. She is focused on engaging Boaz so that he will act the part of the *goel*. He has been very kind to Ruth; he is a man of integrity and honour; and he has a high regard for the Lord and his law. He is a great catch. Perhaps he would serve as kinsman-redeemer.

The agricultural process in ancient Israel is important for the reader to understand the flow of the story. In ancient times this was a five-step process. It began with *ploughing*, which normally took place in the late summer and autumn in anticipation of the winter growing season. The next step was the *sowing of seed*, in which a common practice was for the sower to scatter the seed and then oxen would be driven over the field to trample the seed into the earth. *Harvest* then took place in the spring; as the reader knows from the book of Ruth, reapers cut the stalks of grain and then laid them on the ground. Gleaners tied them together into bundles, and they were then taken to the threshing floor. The fourth step occurred at this floor and it consisted of two parts: the first was *threshing*, in which the grain kernels were separated from the husks; this was usually done with a heavy sledge. The farmer then *winnowed* the mixture in order to collect the heavy grains in one pile and the chaff in another pile. Finally, the grain was taken to the city for storage or for immediate grinding into flour.

The process of threshing and winnowing could take several weeks with a large crop. It was common practice that the owner would stay with and guard his harvest during this time to protect it against theft or fire. According to Naomi, Boaz is working and will be sleeping at the threshing floor this very evening.

Naomi's plan (3:3-4)

With this information in hand, Naomi tells Ruth precisely what to do. In the Hebrew three verbs occur in staccato sequence at the beginning of verse 3: *'Wash ... anoint ... put on...'* Perhaps Ruth is to do these things as a sign that her period of mourning is over.[2] She is now available and ready to be redeemed. This is not seduction. She is to be attractive so that Boaz will understand that she is no longer in mourning and then he can act if he is so interested.

Ruth is then to go to the threshing floor. When Boaz goes to sleep, Ruth is to lie down under the edge of his blanket at his feet. This is the only time in the Bible that the clause to *'uncover his feet'* appears. It has been suggested that this is perhaps a metaphor for sexual activity. There is no evidence to support such an interpretation, and it simply does not fit the story. Naomi's command should be taken at face value, although it is a highly symbolic act. By coming to the threshing floor and lying at Boaz's feet, Ruth is communicating submission. She is, in effect, saying that she wants to be Boaz's wife, and she awaits his judgement and answer in the matter.

One reason that Naomi wants Ruth to approach Boaz this way is because he is a godly man and he would not take advantage of Ruth. He is a man of integrity and he will respond rightly. Boaz knows how to handle such matters. If he is to refuse her, then he will do so in a proper and private way. If rejected, at least Ruth's reputation will be preserved. And that is why Ruth is to wait until Boaz has finished his meal before she presents herself. It is for reasons of privacy. At the mealtime many workers will be there, or round about. Again, this is for privacy and not for seduction. Modern interpreters are often sceptical of this encounter when, in fact, there is no reason to be.

Ruth's obedience (3:5-6)

In a manner consistent with all her prior actions and with her character, Ruth obeys her mother-in-law. The Hebrew of verse 6 underscores this fact: the words translated *'just as'* are in the original language an indication of exactitude.[3] The sense of the passage is 'and she did everything *exactly* as' Naomi had instructed her.

Are their actions in this scene improper? Is Naomi somehow coercing Ruth? Is she manipulating the younger woman to perform immorally? Certainly not! Ruth is being forward, but she is also discreet. She is not compromising her virtue. And, as we shall see, Boaz recognizes that she is approaching him in an honourable way. She is simply attempting to claim her rights under the Mosaic law. There is no scandal here, but privacy keeps disgrace away from both of them. The reality is that Boaz is *not* being manipulated or coerced because he is being approached privately, and not publicly.

Points to ponder

The parallels between the story of Tamar (Gen. 38) and the book of Ruth with regard to the levirate law are extensive and impressive. At some points, however, they diverge and present contrasting images. Tamar, having waited in vain for Judah to

99

fulfil his promise of giving Shelah to her, decides to take action. She removes 'her widow's garments' and covers 'herself with a veil' (Gen. 38:14), and then she sits at the gate of the city of Enaim. Judah, believing her to be a prostitute, engages in sexual activity with her. She is thus impregnated by her father-in-law and bears twin sons who carry on the lineage of her deceased husbands. Although Tamar's intentions might be good, her actions are, to say the least, immoral and sinful.

Tamar is a foil to Ruth. Ruth is in a similar situation to Tamar because she is in need of a kinsman-redeemer to act on her behalf. Ruth, like Tamar, pushes the action. However, there is nothing seedy or questionable about the steps Ruth takes to secure a *goel*. Ruth acts in an upright, honourable way; her behaviour is godly and decent.

This should remind us that good intentions are never enough. Many in the church today have a desire to do good things for the glory of Christ, but are lax and careless as to how they are done. Many have little concern to do things in a godly, right way — the end is all that matters. Then, when things go wrong, the excuse is made: 'I had good intentions!' But the reality is that in Christianity the ends never justify the means.

Chapter 10
At the threshing floor

Please read Ruth 3: 7-13

A number of years ago my family was dealing with the issue of which university my children might attend. The factors that people most commonly take into consideration when making this decision are a widely recognized name, cost, size, availability of suitable living accommodation, what courses are offered, the job market, and how potential employers will regard a degree from a particular institution. In many Christian families, these are the key questions. But ... wait a minute! For a Christian these cannot be the only questions, or even the primary ones. What about seeking God's will in such a decision? Are there good churches in the area? What is the university's perspective on Christianity? Are there on-campus opportunities for Christian fellowship? Are there any Christian professors?

The point of that illustration is that when we have choices or decisions to make, we often act in an earthly-minded way. We are frequently blinded by the world, and so we live by sight. A good biblical example of this conduct is the character of Lot. In Genesis 13, Lot chooses to live in the area of Sodom and Gomorrah. He chooses quickly, and he chooses for the wrong reasons. As J. C. Ryle comments:

He chose by sight and not by faith. He asked no counsel of God, to preserve him from mistakes. He looked to things of time, and not of eternity. He thought of his worldly profit, and not of his soul. He considered only what would help him in this life. He forgot the solemn business of the life to come. This was a bad beginning.[1]

Lot certainly was a believer (2 Peter 2:7-8), yet he was one without the heart of a pilgrim; he lacked the pilgrim spirit.

In our text in this chapter, we shall see that Ruth, on the contrary, does not choose by sight. She is a believer with a pilgrim spirit. She is one who lives by faith.

The opening scene at the threshing floor (3:7)

Now the drama unfolds. Boaz works hard in the fields all day and then, at the close of the day, he has a meal and lies down for the night. There is no indication that he is drunk; when the text says that his heart is *'merry'* it uses a Hebrew word that means 'good', 'happy', or 'satisfied'. Thus, Boaz is content and fulfilled with his day's labour and his evening meal.

Ruth enters the scene and she comes *'softly'*; this latter term actually conveys the idea that she comes to the threshing floor 'in secret', or 'in private'. See, for example, how it is used in 1 Samuel 18:22, where Saul tells his servants to speak to David 'in private'. Ruth then *'uncovered his feet'*. As mentioned earlier, some commentators argue that this expression is some type of euphemism for sexual activity. To be fair, the verb 'to uncover' can be used of a sexual encounter. It is used that way in Leviticus 20:11,17-21. However, the phrase employed there is 'to uncover another's nakedness'. This latter expression is *not* being used in the book of Ruth. Ruth is simply doing what the text says: she is uncovering his feet, lying down at his feet and covering herself with the corner of the blanket.

The great surprise! (3:8-9)

In the middle of the night Boaz is 'startled'; this is a verb that bears the idea of trembling or stuttering. He is at the threshing floor to guard the harvest, and he is not expecting an intruder of this kind. And so he turns himself to look and, 'behold', a woman is lying at his feet. The Hebrew word for 'behold' is a figure of surprise. Boaz is shocked to see and sense that he is not alone under the blanket.

Boaz then asks the woman, 'Who are you?' This question would, of course, make no sense if they were in the midst of a sexual encounter. Ruth answers Boaz with characteristic humility as she twice refers to herself as 'your servant'. Ruth then makes a discreet request of Boaz: 'Spread your wings over your servant.' She is appealing to Boaz to exercise his right as kinsman-redeemer. She is asking him to perform the levirate law and to marry her. The symbol of spreading wings over another person as a sign of marriage and covenant is found in Ezekiel 16:8, in which God says to his people in Jerusalem:

> When I passed by you again and saw you, behold, you were at the age for love, and I spread the corner of my garment [literally, "wing"] over you and covered your nakedness; I made my vow to you and entered into a covenant with you, declares the Lord God, and you became mine.

The word 'wings' appears earlier in the book of Ruth when Boaz wishes Ruth well by saying that she has come under God's

103

'wings' for refuge and protection (2:12). Thus, Ruth is asking that Boaz would be willing to take her under his redemptive wings to protect her. Then the placing of the blanket over her is symbolic of that protection and security.

The blessing of the Lord (3:10)

Here is the second blessing from the Lord that Boaz pronounces on Ruth (see 2:12). Boaz recognizes that Ruth's actions at the threshing floor are even nobler than her earlier deeds on behalf of her mother-in-law. It was wonderful that she left her country and family to follow Naomi, but this is a greater kindness to pursue Boaz as redeemer. Would her desire not be to seek younger, more attractive men? No, Ruth is acting out of deference for her dead husband's family instead of her own desires. She is acting on the voice of piety and not according to her natural inclinations.

Boaz agrees to Ruth's request (3:11-12)

Boaz tells Ruth not to be afraid because he will do all that she has asked of him. Boaz is kind to her. He is not obliged to act, but he assures Ruth that she need not worry. Boaz will act because Ruth is 'a worthy woman', and everyone in Bethlehem is aware of this truth. Boaz actually underscores the reality that the leadership of Bethlehem is knowledgeable about her character. He says, literally, that 'everyone at the gate of my people knows' about Ruth's exemplary character. The gate is the place where the elders sit and make their judgements (see 4:1-2). Yes, indeed, even the elders are keenly aware of Ruth's upright demeanour and life.

Ruth is, in fact, much like Boaz. Back in 2:1, Boaz had been called 'a worthy man'. He is a person of honour, integrity, valour and uprightness. Such language used of both of them certainly argues against the view that this scene at the threshing floor is a seductive and sexually charged situation. No, here is an upright man dealing with an upright woman.

The order of the books in the Hebrew canon is different from that of the English Bible. In the Hebrew canon, the book of Ruth follows the book of Proverbs. In the very last section of Proverbs, the author asks the question, literally: 'A worthy woman who can find?' (Prov. 31:10). Who can find such a woman, of whom it can be said that 'her works praise her in the gates'? (Prov. 31:31). The answer arrives immediately in the Hebrew canon: Boaz found 'a worthy woman'!

It should be further noted that Ruth is not considered a worthy woman because of her outward success. Remember, she is a Moabitess, a widow, a sojourner and childless. She possesses very little outwardly that would cause people to esteem her. Rather, it is her extraordinary character of virtue that brings such esteem from the elders of an Israelite town. The writer of Ecclesiastes is right when he says, 'A good name is better than precious ointment' (Eccles. 7:1).

In verse 12, Boaz mentions an obstacle to the fulfilment of Ruth's request. There is a kinsman-redeemer who is closer to Ruth than Boaz. Hebrew law appears to mandate an order, or rank, among kinsman-redeemers. As noted in an earlier chapter, Leviticus 25:47-49 has a sequence progressing from the closest relative, the brother, to the most distant relative, who is called 'a close relative from his clan'. The latter designation is specifically used of Boaz in the book of Ruth (2:1; 3:2). He is thus not a kinsman of the first rank and, therefore, there is someone ahead of him with a prior right of redemption. The nearer redeemer, then, has the right of first refusal. And thus far the latter has not acted on his rights as *goel*. This has been going on for at least three months, and so Boaz will now push the nearer redeemer into making a decision one way or the other regarding Ruth's situation.

Boaz's final words to Ruth (3:13)

Boaz tells Ruth to *'remain tonight'*. How is the reader to understand this command of Boaz that Ruth should pass the rest of the night at the threshing floor? Obviously, he could not send her to her home in the middle of the night because of possible lurking perils. The gates of the city would probably be shut; there would be danger about; and sentinels or others would certainly see her. So Boaz tells her to *'Lie down until the morning.'* Again, there is no sense of sexual impropriety in this scene; this is for the woman's protection.

Finally, Boaz gives an oath to Ruth. He pledges his word that the next day she will be redeemed. Whether it will be Boaz or the nearer kinsman-redeemer who acts the part is unknown at this point of the story. But, one way or another, redemption will take place. Boaz's vow is serious because it is based on the very existence of God; he says, *'as the Lord* [Yahweh] *lives!'* Boaz gives his word and seals it with an oath employing the covenantal name of the God of Israel.

Points to ponder

1. Seeing things in the long term

Boaz honours Ruth because she did not go after young men,

whether rich or poor. Rather, she sought out the redemption that Boaz could offer and supply. She acts on what is best, and not on what is expedient or exciting. This truth is a lesson for us as undisciplined sinners. We are often driven by what would give us immediate and inward gratification, rather than by what is the right thing to do. Often the right way is hard, laborious, uninteresting, and not worthy of notice. Yet the right way is the choice we ought to make, no matter whether it is glamorous or not.

We face this question daily: do we live by sight or by faith? Do we live a life to glorify Christ or to glorify ourselves? When it comes to our choices, no matter how large or small, we often live by sight and we are drawn by the lustre of the world. The pull of the world is strong and relentless — we often love what it has to offer.

John Newton, the famous pastor and hymn-writer, was one day called to visit a family that had suffered the loss of everything they had as a result of a devastating fire. He found the pious mistress of the house and saluted her with the statement: 'I give you joy, madam!' Surprised and offended, the woman replied, 'What! Joy that all my property has been consumed?' 'Oh no,' Newton answered, 'but joy that you have so much property that fire cannot touch.' This allusion to her real treasure checked the woman's grief and she wiped away her tears. She, as a Christian, knew that what Newton said was true.

May we keep our eyes on the eternal realities, rather than on the fleeting things of the world. May we not be blinded by the mists of the earth, but rather see the heavenly city with clarity. May we live for the good and the right, rather than for the expedient and the charming.

2. Scepticism

The view that the scene at the threshing floor is a sexual encounter appears to be a commonly held position today. My belief is that this perspective reveals more about our day and age than it does about the time of Boaz and Ruth. We live in a sex-sated culture in the West, and so we look back on this story with suspicion and scepticism. We thus read our own mores back into the story. But, in reality, there is nothing in the account that warrants such doubts or reading into the story what is not there.

The irony is that one of the major themes of the book of Ruth is the integrity, honour and uprightness of Boaz and Ruth. They are characters for us to emulate. They are honest, diligent and forthright, and they keep their word.

Chapter 11
Back to Bethlehem

Please read Ruth 3: 14-18

One of the great lessons we learn from the life of Boaz is that he keeps his word and the oaths that he makes. In the section to which we now come Naomi is well aware that promise-keeping is one of Boaz's traits as 'a worthy man'. We ought to take this to heart because we live in a day and age when a person's word is taken and given lightly. We live in a cynical age in which people do not take each other at their word.

The Scottish Covenanters stood and died on their word and oaths. One of their great pledges was 'No king but Jesus'. This oath flew directly in the face of the dominance of England over Scotland in the seventeenth century. England demanded that the Covenanters sign an Oath of Allegiance, which acknowledged the English king to be supreme governor of all persons, and in all causes, both civil and ecclesiastical. Many of the Covenanters refused to sign and, thus, faced the peril of death.

One of the great antagonists against the covenanting church in those days was a cruel, barbaric man named John Graham of Claverhouse. His desire was to destroy every Covenanter. He is well known as the murderer of John Brown. Alexander

Peden said of his friend John Brown, 'Brown was a clear shining light, the greatest Christian I ever conversed with.' Claverhouse attempted to have John Brown take the Oath of Allegiance, but Brown refused to take it, 'declaring as every true Covenanter did that they knew no king but Jesus Christ'.[1] Claverhouse then said to Brown, 'Go to your prayers, for you are going to die.' Brown's prayer was so moving that Claverhouse's soldiers refused to lift a hand against him. So Claverhouse killed Brown himself.

After the dreadful deed was done, Claverhouse turned to Isabel Brown and said, 'What thinkest of thy husband now, woman?' She replied, 'I thought much good of him, and now more than ever.' Like Boaz and like Brown, when we give our word we ought to keep our word — it is our very bond, even unto death.

The remainder of the night (3:14)

Ruth lies at Boaz's feet until the morning. This is a humble place; it is a place of submission — and yet a place of protection. She is not, however, next to him in the place of the wife. Thus the drama continues to unfold: will Ruth become Boaz's wife, or not? Will she be able to come fully under the blanket, or not?

Ruth then arises early in the morning while it is still dark. She does this *before one could recognize another*. In other words, the field workers will soon begin to stir, and they will start to arrive at the threshing floor to make preparations for the work of the day. They may, of course, draw the wrong conclusions if they see Ruth under Boaz's blanket. This would probably be seen as inappropriate and scandalous, even though the activity there has truly been above board.

Boaz realizes the danger of rumour and gossip. Nothing that he and Ruth have done is wrong, but he is concerned about how people might view it. The scene could develop into scandal, and Boaz wants to protect Ruth's good reputation. And, thus, Boaz makes a general comment: 'Let it not be known that the woman came to the threshing floor.' This is perhaps an internal speech; he is speaking to his own heart to guard what he says and to protect Ruth from scandal. Or it may be that some of the workers are nearby, and perhaps Boaz is commanding them not to speak of what they have seen.

In the morning (3:15)

Before Ruth returns to Naomi, Boaz tells her to spread out her 'garment' so that he can fill it with barley that has been threshed at the floor. This article of clothing is an outer cloak that she had worn to the threshing floor (cf. Isa. 3:22). Boaz places 'six measures of barley' in the cloak that Ruth holds out. The term 'measure' is undefined with regard to capacity or weight, but the fact that there are six portions appears to underscore that it is an ample, if not an abundant, amount of barley.

It has been argued by a few commentators that this provision may be a payment for prostitution. How absurd! This act is not merely a provision, and it is certainly not remuneration for sexual favours. It is, in reality, a pledge from Boaz to Ruth that he will act in the matter of redemption. The barley, then, is a token that he will indeed serve as her redeemer and marry her if he can work out the logistics that very day.

Multiple ancient manuscripts, including the Syriac and Vulgate versions, translate the last sentence of the verse as 'Then she went into the city.' Many modern translations, such as the ESV, accept and follow that rendition. However, the Hebrew text actually reads, 'Then he went into the city.' The latter translation makes

111

perfectly good sense: as soon as Boaz gives his word to Ruth, he immediately and directly goes to Bethlehem to fulfil his oath. There is no lingering on his part. He is diligent to bring the matter to a conclusion, and thus keep his word.

Ruth reports to Naomi (3:16-17)

Ruth now returns to her mother-in-law, and Naomi questions her about how things went at the threshing floor. Ruth gives her an account of the proceedings, and then shows her the six measures of barley Boaz had given to her. The grain serves as a token and pledge, not only to Ruth, but to Naomi as well. It is a visible sign of his promise. Of course, it also has a utilitarian purpose of providing food for a household in need.

Ruth closes her account to Naomi by quoting Boaz. He had given the barley to Ruth, and then said to her that it would not be right for her to return to Naomi 'empty-handed'. This is the same word that was used back in 1:21, where Naomi declares that the Lord has brought her back to Bethlehem 'empty'. Thus, no longer will she be 'empty', but Naomi now has Boaz's pledge that redemption will come this very day. The fullness of the grain pledge points to the fullness of Boaz's promise.

Naomi's conclusion (3:18)

Naomi understands the significance of the grain as a pledge, or token, of Boaz's word. She knows that he is a man of integrity, and that he will 'not rest' until the matter is brought to its proper conclusion. So her advice to Ruth is to have patience and wait to see how it will turn out. They will not have to wait for long, but the matter will be resolved 'today'.

112

Boaz is prompt and industrious. He will take care of the issue of redemption, even at a time when his business affairs are so demanding. The work at the threshing floor is urgent and pressing, but Boaz will first take care of the matter of Ruth. This demonstrates where his heart is. The affair of doing what is right for Ruth is more important than any business.

The drama of the story is now at a fever pitch. We yearn to learn the outcome of it. What will happen in the city? How will Boaz work out the situation? How will the nearest kinsman respond? We anticipate a wonderful ending to the story. However, we also anticipate something greater because we know that the climax of the story is not the redemption of Ruth by Boaz, but rather the coming of the true redeemer. It is through Boaz and Ruth that this seed will come — the seed that points to David, the great king of Israel, and to his progeny Jesus, the greatest king of Israel!

Points to ponder

Boaz is a man of his word. Christians ought to be people who stand behind their word, no matter what the consequences. A good example of one who kept his oath to the Lord, and did not give his oath to another, is the Rev. John Livingstone. He was a member of the Westminster Assembly in the 1640s, while he pastored a church in Ireland. Within twenty years of the Assembly, some of the divines were thrown out of their churches because they would not sign the Oath of Allegiance; this occurred in 1662 and it was called 'the Great Ejectment', or 'Ejection'.

At this time, Livingstone was brought before the ecclesiastical council in Edinburgh and, according to his own words:

113

... they required me to subserve [i.e. subscribe to] the oath which they called the Oath of Allegiance, wherein the king was to be acknowledged supreme governor over all persons, and in all causes, both civil and ecclesiastical. This I know was contrived ... that it might import [i.e. bring about] receding from the covenant for reformation, and the bringing in of the bishops... Therefore, I refused to take that oath. They desired to know if I would take some time to advise anent [i.e. to consider] the matter, as some who had been before them had done... I told I needed not take time, seeing I was abundantly clear that I could not lawfully take that oath.[2]

Livingstone had given his word to the covenant and to King Jesus, and he would not break that oath.

And there were consequences. The ecclesiastical council pronounced banishment for him. Livingstone was given forty-eight hours to vacate Edinburgh, and two months to leave all the king's domains. He left his church and fled to Rotterdam. Within a year, his wife came to him with two of their children, although five children remained in Scotland. Livingstone, a Scottish lion of the covenant, died in Rotterdam on 9 August 1672. Livingstone paid a heavy price for keeping his word, and perhaps one day we too shall be called to stand by our pledge at great cost to ourselves.

Part 5:
Redemption (3: 1-22)

Chapter 12
The courtroom scene

Please read Ruth 4: 1-12

The passage to which we now come clearly teaches that a good name and good reputation are abiding values. Scripture often teaches that truth. Ecclesiastes 7:1, for instance, says, 'A good name is better than precious ointment.' Being a noble, courageous person who is esteemed by others is better than owning expensive perfume because good character is more lasting and valuable than material riches. Proverbs 22:1 echoes that truth when it says, 'A good name is to be chosen rather than great riches.' As quoted earlier, C. H. Spurgeon poignantly states, 'A good character is the best tombstone. Those who loved you, and were helped by you, will remember you. So carve your name on hearts, and not on marble.'

The following story told by R. C. Sproul is appropriate here. There was a young man who was eager to go and fight in a great battle. He was under age and had to sneak away from home to join the troops. But he was successful and joined the army. As the battle began, the young man was overcome with fear. He had never expected war to be like this. And so he ran away. His commanding officer sent soldiers to find him and bring him back. When the young man returned, he was taken to the king. The king demanded to know his name. But the young man only mumbled a response. The king grew angrier and said, 'Young man, what is your name?' The young man then said, 'Alexander, Your Majesty.' With that King Alexander the Great shouted at the frightened young man, 'Alexander? Young man, either change your name or change your behaviour!'

At the gate (4:1)

Boaz has left the threshing floor, enters into Bethlehem and now sits down in the area of 'the gate'. Why does he take up a position there? In antiquity this was the place where legal matters were decided by the elders of the city. Excavations at Iron Age sites in Israel have uncovered a number of gateways with built-in benches where the elders would sit in judgement (such as at Megiddo and Gezer). The elders met at the gate because it was the focus of great activity in an ancient town: traders with goods and news first came through the gate area; often the central square or piazza of the town would be situated right next to the gate. In any event, Boaz sits in the gate area, and this act may be a sign that he is an important figure in Bethlehem, perhaps an elder of the town.

People commonly pass through this area and, 'behold', the nearest kinsman-redeemer comes walking by. The timing, of course, is perfect. And so Boaz addresses the man, and he calls him 'friend'. This word in Hebrew is quite vague, and it literally means 'whoever', or 'such and such'. Why is the man's name not given? Perhaps it is a mark of shame. He has not done his duty with regard to redemption, and so he brings disrepute on his own name. Ironically, the man is attempting to preserve his own name (see 4:6), but in the end he remains nameless. In other words, he has simply become another 'such and such' (cf. 1 Sam. 21:2; 2 Kings 6:8).

118

On the contrary, Boaz's name is mentioned twice in this verse.[1] Remember, Boaz's name literally means, 'In him is strength' (see comments on 2:1). What a contrast to this man who is Mr 'Such and such'!

The setting of the courtroom (4:2)

Boaz then gathers ten elders of Bethlehem, and he tells them to sit at the gate. These men are to sit in judgement over the case that Boaz will present (see Deut. 21:18-19; 22:13-15). The number 'ten' may signify what is needed for a judicial quorum. In later Jewish practice during the Roman period, ten men were required to be present for a synagogue service to be held. The number ten in Hebrew culture often also symbolizes a state of completion and finality. Thus, Boaz is expecting a conclusive and binding judgement to be given by the court in the case before them.

We are witnessing, therefore, a courtroom scene, in which a case will be presented and a judgement will be accorded. We get to see the judicial proceedings of a town in early Iron Age Israel and how the system operates.

Boaz's case (4:3-4)

Boaz now presents his case to the court, which includes the elders, the nearest kinsman-redeemer and onlookers. He explains, first of all, that Naomi has returned from Moab, and she is planning to sell the land that belongs to Elimelech in the area of Bethlehem. The reason that Naomi wants to sell the property is because the grain harvests are now almost over, and she has no other means of support or subsistence. Apparently if

119

Naomi is indigent, she has every right to sell the land in order to survive. Leviticus 25:25 says, 'If your brother becomes poor and sells part of his property...'

Land that is sold for this reason is not to be sold in perpetuity; rather, the land is eventually to revert to the clan and to the tribes to whom the Lord had originally allotted the property (Lev. 25:23-24). It is the kinsman-redeemer who has the duty to make certain that the land is brought back into the family structure. Leviticus 25:25 continues, '... then his nearest redeemer shall come and redeem what his brother has sold.' The question that Boaz brings before the court at the gate of Bethlehem is whether the nearest goel will act on this matter, and perform his duty, or not. The situation of the possible land sale is forcing the hand of the nearest kinsman-redeemer. The man's response is immediate: 'I will redeem it' (4:4).

An example parallel to what is going on in Ruth 4 can be seen in Jeremiah 32:6-15. In that passage, Hanamel, who is Jeremiah's cousin, decides to sell a field that is in the area of Anathoth. Jeremiah is the closest goel and has 'the right of possession and redemption' (v. 8). Jeremiah responds by purchasing the field so that it stays in the possession of the family. The legal steps of Jeremiah's procurement of the land are stated in verse 10: 'I signed the deed, sealed it, got witnesses, and weighed the money on scales.' He presents the sealed deed 'in the presence of the witnesses who signed the deed of purchase, and in the presence of all the Judeans who were sitting in the court of the guard' (v. 12).

Why does Boaz begin with the issue of the redemption of the land, rather than with the redemption of Ruth? It is uncertain why he does this, although perhaps the matter of land carries with it a stronger legal obligation than the issue of the

120

redemption of a foreign woman. Or, maybe, it would be seen as unseemly, or indiscreet, in Hebrew culture for Boaz to begin discussions with the topic of a woman. Others argue that Boaz is simply being shrewd in his dealings, and he is setting a trap for the nearest redeemer. In other words, perhaps Boaz is well aware of the man's circumstances, and so he lures him in order to get proper closure to the judicial case. In any event, Boaz is forcing the nearest *goel* to make a decision.

The pivot (4:5-6)

Boaz then reveals to the court that for the nearest kinsman to acquire the land by redemption he will also have to act on the levirate law with regard to Ruth. It is his duty to marry the widow of his deceased kinsman, and to raise seed in the name of the dead relative (Deut. 25:5-6). Why is this the case? Could the *goel* not simply redeem the land and not the woman? We do not know the answer for certain. Perhaps it was a binding legal obligation to perform a full redemption — that is, everything must be redeemed. Or perhaps Naomi had made it a condition of the land purchase: if someone buys the land, he must also redeem Ruth.

The news that Ruth is included in the transaction is a deal-killer. The closest *goel* changes his mind. He says, '*I cannot redeem it*', both at the beginning and the end of his reply. This is an *inclusio* that serves to emphasize his negative response, and it is the exact opposite of what he had said in verse 4, when he had stated, 'I will redeem it.'

The man's change of heart is because he might '*impair [his] own inheritance*'. He believes that the redemption would be too costly and dear for him. Why? One common thought is that

121

the man is concerned that a son born to him and Ruth would share the inheritance already planned for his own children. Another possibility is that if the man is childless and has no heir, then all of his own estate would pass on to the child of the levirate union. And the mother is a Moabite to boot! In any event, the nearest kinsman-redeemer believes that he would be acting against his own interests, and so he bows out of the process.

The door is now wide open for Boaz to act as redeemer.

The sign of the sandal (4:7-8)

Now that Boaz has received the right of redemption, he seeks to seal the deal. The author of the book of Ruth describes a practice common in the days of the judges as a means of confirming an agreement between two parties. The confirmation of a transaction is done by one person taking off his sandal and giving it to another. What does this act symbolize? We are not certain. However, the shoe may be a sign of power, authority and ownership. For example, in Deuteronomy 11:24, God says to Israel, 'Every place on which the sole of your foot treads shall be yours.' 'This may perhaps refer to the practice of gaining formal title to a land by walking through it'[2] (cf. Josh. 1:3; 14:9). Thus, when the *goel* takes off his sandal and passes it to Boaz, he is yielding and transferring his land rights to Boaz. In this regard, the gesture is a sign, or symbol, of an agreement, or, as the text calls it, *'the manner of attesting'.*

And so the closest kinsman turns to Boaz and says, *'Buy it for yourself.'* Then he takes off his sandal and, according to some early translations, like the Septuagint, 'he gave it to Boaz'. The

122

man, therefore, gives his word and then performs a symbolic act to seal and give witness to the spoken word.

Witnesses (4:9-10)

Boaz now formally takes acquisition of all that belongs to Elimelech and his sons, Chilion and Mahlon. Human witnesses are necessary to confirm this transaction. So Boaz calls on the elders sitting at the gate, and the other people who have gathered to watch the proceedings, to testify to this deal. It is a legal assembly called on to attest and to validate the oath and the covenant that has been made. This was a common form of notarization in ancient Israel (see Josh. 24:22; 1 Sam. 12:5). The transaction is also legally validated by reference to a date. In verse 9, the text includes the timing of 'this day' or, literally, 'today'. Old Testament contracts commonly include a date of validation (see Gen. 31:48). The use of the term 'today' also fulfils Naomi's declaration to Ruth at the end of chapter 3 that 'the man will not rest but will settle the matter today' (3:18).

It should be noted that the order of the names of Elimelech's sons is reversed from earlier in the story (see 1:2). Why the reversal? The author is simply placing in the last position the name of the one who is of most importance to the subsequent narrative. Thus the next verse begins, '*Also Ruth the Moabite, the widow of Mahlon...*' (4:10).

In verse 10 Boaz formally takes Ruth as his wife and he announces his intention to perform the levirate law (according to Deut. 25:6). The legal nature of this scene is highlighted by Boaz calling Ruth 'Ruth, the Moabite, the widow of Mahlon...' Boaz is detailed in presenting his case; it is similar to a modern courtroom scene in which a person is called on to 'state your full name' to the court. In addition, Boaz ends his courtroom speech the same way that he began it, by saying, *'You are witnesses this day'* (4:9,10). This is an *inclusio* that emphatically calls the people who are present to affirm what they have seen and heard. Boaz is careful to make certain that all the legal proceedings are carried out in a proper and upright way.

At the beginning of verse 9, Boaz announces that he has purchased *'all that belonged to Elimelech'*. What a contrast to the first kinsman-redeemer, who thought it would be too costly for him to redeem it all! Boaz, on the other hand, appears to exult in all that he has acquired.

The chorus (4:11-12)

The two groups of spectators from verse 9, 'the elders and all the people', now respond to Boaz and his call that they should be witnesses to the transaction. In verse 11, however, the two groups are reversed, as it says, *'all the people ... and the elders'.* This is a chiastic structure for the purpose of emphasis; indeed, everyone who had seen the courtroom case will now bear witness to its legality and validity. The response of the community, in the original text, is merely one word: 'Witnesses!' It is as if they are all speaking this one word in unison. This underscores the unity of the people in their answer. All are in agreement!

The community then pronounces a three-part blessing on Boaz and Ruth.

The opening part of the blessing is the hope that the Lord will cause Ruth to be *'like Rachel and Leah'*. Rachel and Leah were sisters, the daughters of Laban (Gen. 29 – 30). The patriarch Jacob had married both of them, and they, along with their concubines, gave birth to the twelve sons of Jacob. Of course, these twelve sons were the progenitors of the twelve tribes of Israel. Verse 11 says of the two sisters that they 'together built up the house of Israel'. The personal name 'Israel' in this text refers both to Jacob, whose name was changed to Israel (Gen. 32:28), and to the nation consisting of the twelve tribes.

Rachel is mentioned before Leah although the latter is the older of the two. The reason for this order is that Rachel was the beloved wife of Jacob. This is obvious from a text like Genesis 33:1-2, in which Jacob is about to face danger, and so he places Rachel right at the rear of his people as they advance. As the rabbis comment, 'The more behind — the more beloved!'

The next part of the blessing calls for Boaz to 'act worthily in Ephrathah' (this is another name for Bethlehem). The word used for 'worthily' is hayil in Hebrew, and it has already been used for Boaz (2:1) and for Ruth (3:11). Thus, this blessing is calling for Boaz to continue to act with integrity and honour in a way that he has already demonstrated in his life.

The people further proclaim that they hope that Boaz will 'be renowned in Bethlehem'. The text literally says, 'May the name be called in Bethlehem'; in other words, may Boaz's name become famous in the history of the town. The whole point here is that the people anticipate that Boaz's life and actions will speak volumes to others. May Boaz have a good name and a good reputation!

The final part of the people's blessing is seen in verse 12. They wish that Boaz's house may be 'like the house of Perez, whom Tamar bore to Judah'. As mentioned earlier, this refers to Genesis 38. There are many similarities between the stories of Tamar and Ruth. Both women are foreign (Tamar is an Adullamite), and both resort to the levirate law to continue the lines of descent for their deceased husbands. And both perpetuate the family lines in the tribe of Judah. The people of Bethlehem are from that tribe and are largely descended through the line of Perez. Thus, the reference here is specially relevant to them.

Points to ponder

Some commentators and preachers are quick to conclude that, throughout the story of Ruth, Boaz is a type of Christ. In other words, many understand this story principally as a picture of the work of Jesus in redeeming sinners. The picture looks something like this: the return from Moab of Naomi (and Ruth) in destitute circumstances and bitterness represents each one of us as a fallen, sinful creature. Ruth then goes to the field searching for a redeemer; all sinners are to search for one who can deliver them. Ruth finds Boaz as redeemer, and he is kind to her and saves her from her poor, bitter and hard life. This, of course, is seen as a picture of Jesus having compassion on sinners who come to him for deliverance, and he gives them newness of life. Again, many read the book of Ruth in a like manner.

So, is Boaz a type of Christ? Probably not. I am very hesitant in drawing such a conclusion because Scripture itself never makes the connection between the two figures. A clear type is found, for example, in Romans 5:14, which says, 'Adam ... was a type of the one who was to come.' We never see anything in the Bible that ties Jesus to Boaz in a similar way. Thus, I am sceptical and believe we need to be careful in making Boaz some type of Christ-figure. He does, however, exhibit some Christlike behaviour. He demonstrates compassion and kindness, and performs his redemptive duty well.

126

Does that position on the relationship between Boaz and Jesus dull the Christological significance and intent of the book of Ruth? By no means! The very purpose of the book is to demonstrate and underscore God's providence in the coming of the Messiah through the lineage of Ruth and Boaz. That point will be further driven home by the study of the very last section of the book.

Chapter 13
The descendant

Please read Ruth 4: 13-22

One of the great motifs of Scripture is how God repeatedly preserves the seed and line of the Messiah from what appears to be certain extinction. Though Satan and his minions would seek to wipe out the Messianic line over and over again, God remains faithful to deliver it and sustain it. The promise of Genesis 3:15 will come to pass because of the sovereign work and protection of God. So, even though Cain kills Abel, God raises up a replacement in Seth; though Pharaoh attempts to destroy the people of Israel, God establishes a deliverer in Moses; though many nations rage against, and attempt to demolish, Israel during the period of the judges, God responds by saving his people by the hand of various deliverers. And, indeed, all that happened in the lives of Ruth and Boaz serves to bring about the Lord's redemptive plans for his people because through their lineage the Messiah would come. This all testifies to God's providence, plan and sovereignty. He controls everything and uses it to accomplish his good ends.

What a wonderful truth! In 1776 John Newton wrote the following to a Mrs Place:

I will tell you then, though you know it, that the Lord reigns. He who once bore our sins, and carried our sorrows, is seated upon a throne of glory, and exercises all power in heaven and on earth. Thrones, principalities, and powers, bow before him. Every event in the kingdoms of providence and of grace is under his rule. His providence pervades and manages the whole, and is as minutely attentive to every part, as if there were only that single object in his view. From the tallest archangel to the meanest ant or fly, all depend on him for their being, their preservation, and their powers. He directs the sparrows where to build their nests, and to find their food. He overrules the rise and fall of nations, and bends, with an invincible energy and unerring wisdom, all events; so that, while many intend nothing less, in the issue, their designs all concur and coincide in the accomplishment of his holy will. He restrains with a mighty hand the still more formidable efforts of the powers of darkness; and Satan, with all his hosts, cannot exert their malice a hair's breadth beyond the limits of his permission. This is he who is the head and husband of his believing people.

Marriage and birth (4:13)

Here we see the conclusion to all that has gone before. Everything in the story is now coming to an initial climax. Ruth and Boaz marry; the marriage is consummated; and the Lord opens Ruth's womb to conceive. Thus we view the human story coming to a happy and joyous end. Ruth is no longer a sojourner, or one of Boaz's servants (2:13), but now she is his 'wife'. All that is good as far as it goes. However, we need to understand that there is another, greater, story in this book. And that larger story will not be concluded until verses 18-22. Thus we ought to anticipate a greater fulfilment to the story later in the chapter.

We need to take note again of God's sovereignty in this story. The text literally says, 'And Yahweh gave to her conception.' In other words, it is the Lord, according to the counsel of his immutable and righteous will, who opens Ruth's womb for conception. In his providence, he causes a child to be born for his own purpose and glory. It is the Lord who graciously and mercifully provides for Ruth again. His grace is clearly underlined because the child is a son; here is the male heir who is to carry on the family name and the rights of inheritance.

Blessing on Naomi (4:14-15)

In reaction to the birth of a son, the women of Bethlehem pronounce a blessing on Naomi. This group, or chorus, first appeared in the story back in 1:19. There Naomi had just returned from Moab, and the women, perhaps with a vicious slur, had asked, 'Is this Naomi?' Things have changed indeed from that time to this!

Why is Naomi the one being addressed here, and not Ruth? Ruth is now cared for because she is in the family of Boaz. Naomi, on the other hand, is in need of a grandson who will inherit and continue the line of Elimelech. Naomi's hope lies in the offspring of Ruth and Boaz; here is one who will be heir and take care of her in her old age.

Now let us consider the content of the women's blessing on Naomi. They begin by praising God: 'Blessed be the Lord ...!' May his name be praised because he has provided a redeemer for the family of Elimelech; the *goel* mentioned in this verse is not Boaz, but rather his son. The Lord has given Naomi a redeemer. If he had not been born, the land and inheritance of Elimelech would have gone to Boaz's family and Elimelech's name would not have been preserved. The child, then, is truly a *goel* — that is, a true heir of Elimelech's inheritance.

The women then exclaim, '*... may his name be renowned in Israel!*' (4:14). Grammatically, the word 'his' could refer either to the Lord or to Naomi's grandson. However, the following verse (4:15) clearly speaks of the child who has been born to Ruth, and so it is a continuation of the male child as the subject of verse 14. A similar blessing was given earlier by the people at the gate with regard to Boaz (4:11). But there is a distinction. Whereas the people at the gate call for Boaz to become famous 'in Bethlehem', the women call for the child to have a great name '*in Israel*'. The wish and blessing of the women are for the child to have an even wider influence and impact than his father.

In verse 15, the blessing pronounced by the women continues. First, they hope that the child will be '*a restorer of life*' to Naomi. The term for '*life*' used here can simply mean 'soul'. Remember how Naomi had returned from Moab: she was in bitter circumstances, in poverty, and in an apparently hopeless condition. Ruth's son, however, brings hope, redemption and newness. Ironically, the word translated '*restorer*' is literally 'returner'; it is from the same verb that is used twice in 1:22, in which Naomi and Ruth 'returned' from the land of Moab. Naomi has returned to Israel, and the child born to Ruth will 'return' her life to her!

The women also pray that the heir will be a '*nourisher of your old age*'. This is simply expressing the desire that the child will care for Naomi in her old age, infirmity and her death and burial. The verb employed is often used in Hebrew of supplying another person with food and the necessities of life. Naomi had come back from Moab 'empty' (1:21), but now may this child reverse that circumstance.

132

Naomi has already been greatly blessed because Ruth loves her and has stood by her through thick and thin. In fact, the women of Bethlehem claim that having Ruth is better than having seven sons. This is an astounding compliment; it is high praise, especially in the context of this family which has so eagerly anticipated the birth of a male heir. How highly valued sons are in Hebrew culture! Yet Ruth is better than 'seven' sons; that number in Hebrew often symbolizes fullness and completion. Who could ask for more than seven sons? Yet Ruth is better than even that blessing.

Naomi and the child (4:16)

Naomi tenderly takes the child, and places him on her own lap. This is a symbolic gesture. Some have argued that it is a formal rite of adoption, but the biblical evidence in support of that is rather weak (cf. Gen. 50:23). In reality, it is a symbol that Naomi views the child as her own in a manner of speaking. He is the heir of her husband's estate and the continuance of her husband's line — almost as though Naomi had produced the child herself.

The text then says that Naomi 'became his nurse'. The Hebrew term for 'nurse' often bears the sense of someone being one who takes care of another. It is used, for example, in 2 Kings 10:1-5 of those who are guardians of the royal household. Perhaps Naomi continues to live with Ruth and Boaz, and thus she takes on some responsibility for the care of the child.

The naming (4:17)

The female neighbours in Bethlehem not only bless Naomi, but

133

they name the child. In Scripture, the father is normally the one who names children, and sometimes the mother does so (1 Sam. 1:20). Why do the women name the child in this instance? The birth of the male heir has obviously become an event in which the whole town is involved! There has been much participation by the town in the marriage of Boaz and Ruth; many of the townspeople had been at the gate and had served as witnesses to the redemptive process. Now many of the women of Bethlehem fully participate in the naming of the child.

They give the name 'Obed' to the boy. In Hebrew, this word is a participle that literally means 'one serving'. A Hebrew participle indicates an ongoing, continuous action. The idea is that the child will provide aid to Naomi now and into the future. His birth preserves the line and inheritance of Elimelech, Naomi's deceased husband. In this sense, Obed 'has been born to Naomi'.

Obed's service goes well beyond the immediate story of Ruth, Naomi and Boaz. The importance of Obed's lineage is emphasized as the author tells us that Obed will one day be the father of Jesse and the grandfather of David. Therefore, through Obed came the greatest king in the history of Israel; in that regard Obed is truly a servant of the kingdom! Thus, the storyline broadens. On one level we are witnessing the history of Naomi, Ruth, Boaz and Obed. But there is a second, higher, tier to the account, and that is the story that leads to David, the man after God's own heart, and the work of God whose providence brought him to the throne of Israel. The royal line of Israel came through this unlikely pairing of Ruth and Boaz!

But there is an even broader and higher tier to the story. For we know that through David's line will come the Messiah. We read the following in Luke's genealogy of Jesus: '... the son of Melea, the son of Menna, the son of Mattatha, the son of Nathan,

134

the son of David, the son of Jesse, the son of Obed, the son of Boaz' (Luke 3:31-32). We are to be struck by the way that this small story of Ruth and Boaz fits into the unfolding of God's revelational history. God's sovereignty and providence are at work; indeed, history is 'his story'.

The trajectory (4:18-22)

In verse 17, the author gave us a short, simple genealogical statement that Obed fathered Jesse, and Jesse fathered David. The present section is a broader genealogy that traces the descent from seven generations before Obed and then concludes with David. Why does the author begin the genealogy with Perez? In Genesis 38, Perez was born to Judah in the affair with Tamar. It was to Judah that God had promised a royal line through the blessing that Jacob had given to his son. Jacob's blessing to Judah is as follows:

Judah, your brothers shall praise you;
> your hand shall be on the neck of your enemies;
> your father's sons shall bow down before you.
Judah is a lion's cub;
> from the prey, my son, you have gone up.
He stooped down; he crouched as a lion
> and as a lioness; who dares rouse him?
The sceptre shall not depart from Judah,
> nor the ruler's staff from between his feet,
until tribute comes to him;
> and to him shall be the obedience of the peoples
> (Gen. 49:8-10).

The kingly line, according to Jacob, will proceed through the lineage of Judah. Judah's son by Tamar is Perez, and it is through the line of Perez that the genealogy concludes with King David.

135

The genealogy is selective. It does not list every generation or descendant from Perez to David. Most genealogies in the Bible are not exhaustive; they list only certain names and they are also highly structured. The genealogy in this passage lists ten names. The number ten in Hebrew culture often denotes completion and fulfilment (e.g., the ten plagues, the Ten Commandments, etc.). The idea of the structure before us is that the kingly promise to Judah reaches its climax and crescendo in the appearance of David, the great king of Israel from the tribe of Judah.

This genealogy is almost exactly what is recorded in the genealogy of Jesus in Matthew 1:3-6. The point of its inclusion is so that the reader should understand that the genealogy in Ruth actually finds its ultimate climax in the coming of the Messiah, Jesus Christ. Observe how the main characters have faded from the story. Boaz and Ruth are now out of the picture; theirs is not the main story. The emphasis now is the lineage that points to Christ. The coming of the Messiah is the end-all of the book of Ruth.

Points to ponder

When they consider the doctrine of the sovereignty of God, many people, in reality, hold to a macro-sovereignty — that is, they believe that huge events and matters come to pass because of God's plan and work. However, the proposition that *everything* comes to pass as a result of the sovereignty and providence of God is not widely believed. A full and proper view of divine sovereignty requires an understanding that everything, no matter how large or small, has an appointed time in God's plan and purpose (Eccles. 3:1-8). Matthew Henry comments: 'Those things which to us seem most casual and contingent are in the counsel and foreknowledge of God, punctually determined, and the very hour of them is fixed, and can neither be anticipated nor adjourned a moment.'

The *Westminster Larger Catechism* agrees when it asks and answers the following question:

What are the decrees of God?

God's decrees are the wise, free, and holy acts of the counsel of his will, whereby, from all eternity, he hath, for his own glory, unchangeably foreordained whatsoever comes to pass in time, especially concerning angels and men.[1]

The episode involving Ruth and Boaz illustrates the correct perspective on the sovereignty of God. This is a story of the lives of a few characters in a short period of time and in a small geographical setting. And yet God uses them to accomplish much higher purposes. Indeed, they help to establish the line of the Messiah, the promised seed of the woman!

This truth should be a good lesson to all Christians. All believers serve a greater purpose than merely what goes on in their immediate lives. Christians are part of a greater scheme of God's unfolding plan and purpose for his church. And so, let us not think and ponder only of the here and now, and let us not only act for the present, but may we have eyes of eternity and live according to eternal realities!

Notes

Introduction
1. T. Paine, *Age of Reason* (Secaucus, NJ, 1991), p.121. Cited in V. P. Hamilton, *Handbook on the Historical Books* (Grand Rapids: Baker, 2000), pp.187-8.
2. R. L. Hubbard, *The Book of Ruth*, New International Commentary on the Old Testament (Grand Rapids: Eerdmans, 1989), pp.23-35.

Chapter 1 — The setting of suffering (1:1-5)
1. A. Dallimore, *George Whitefield: The Life and Times of the Great Evangelist of the Eighteenth Century Revival*, vol. 1 (London: Banner of Truth, 1970), p.145.
2. F. Brown, S. R. Driver and C. A. Briggs, *A Hebrew and English Lexicon of the Old Testament* (Oxford: Clarendon Press, 1907, pp.6534).
3. *Ibid.*, p.479.
4. L. Koehler and W. Baumgartner, *Lexicon in Veteris Testamenti Libros* (Leiden: Brill, 1985), p.738.
5. Brown, Driver and Briggs, *Hebrew and English Lexicon*, p.946.

Chapter 2 — Graciousness in the midst of suffering (1:6-9)
1. John D. Currid, *Why Do I Suffer? Suffering and the Sovereignty of God* (Ross-shire: Christian Focus, 2004), pp.53-4.
2. Thomas Watson, *A Divine Cordial: Romans 8:28* (J. P. Green Pub., 2001 reprint), p.21.

Chapter 3 — Orpah and Ruth respond (1:10-14)
1. A. W. Pink, *The Attributes of God* (Grand Rapids, MI: Baker, 1975 reprint), p.40.
2. Quoted in M. W. Tileston, *Daily Strength for Daily Needs* (Boston: Little, Brown & Co., 1884), p.67.

3. The English Standard Version translates this word as a negative. It can have that sense at times, but that is rare.
4. Currid, *Why Do I Suffer?*, p.13.
5. *Westminster Confession of Faith*, V:5.

Chapter 5 — Homecoming (1:19-22)

1. B. B. Warfield, 'Predestination', in *A Dictionary of the Bible*, ed. J. Hastings, vol. 4 (New York: Charles Scribner's Sons, 1909), pp.47-63.
2. *Westminster Confession*, V:1.
3. J. Currid, *The Expectant Prophet: Habakkuk Simply Explained* (Darlington: Evangelical Press, 2009), p.66. This story is originally found in J. Purves, *Fair Sunshine* (Edinburgh: Banner of Truth, 1985).
4. W. A. VanGemeren, ed., *New International Dictionary of Old Testament Theology and Exegesis*, vol. 4 (Grand Rapids: Zondervan, 1997), p.47.
5. The parallel here may be stronger than this translation based on the ESV suggests. The verb 'testified' may, in fact, be better translated as 'afflicted'. The Greek Old Testament (the Septuagint) clearly understands it that way.
6. Currid, *Why Do I Suffer?*, pp. 113-14.
7. A. W. Pink, *Gleanings in Joshua* (Chicago: Moody Press, 1981), p.79.

Chapter 6 — Ruth gleans in the fields (2:1-7)

1. John Calvin, *Institutes of the Christian Religion* (Grand Rapids: Eerdmans, 1981), Book 1, ch. xvi, sect. 8, p.179.
2. Hubbard, *The Book of Ruth*, pp.150-52.

Chapter 7 — Conversations between Ruth and Boaz (2:8-17)

1. The verbal stem used by the author has the sense of easing one's pain.
2. The stem of this verb, 'to glean', in Hebrew is intensive, and the form of the verb is probably a jussive (i.e., expressing a command). This is, indeed, a command to be obeyed.
3. J. Currid, 'Weights and Measures', in T. D. Alexander and D. W. Baker, eds., *Dictionary of the Old Testament: Pentateuch* (Downers Grove, IL: InterVarsity Press, 2003), p.889.

Chapter 8 — Ruth reports to Naomi (2:18-23)

1. Brown, Driver and Briggs, *Hebrew and English Lexicon*, p.145.
2. Such as the Vulgate and the Syriac Old Testament.
3. See the discussion of the verb 'take notice of', or 'recognize', in the comments on 2:10.

140

4. E. F. Campbell Jr., *Ruth,* The Anchor Bible, vol. 7 (New York: Doubleday, 1975), p.106.
5. Hubbard, *The Book of Ruth*, p.182, n.7.

Chapter 9 — Naomi's plan (3:1-6)
1. See C. Westermann, 'Structure and Intention of the Book of Ruth', *Word and World*, no. 19 (1999), pp.285-302.
2. As is the case later for David — see 2 Samuel 12:20.
3. This is an example of *kaph-veritatis,* a construction that signifies absolute precision.

Chapter 10 — At the threshing floor (3:7-13)
1. J. C. Ryle, *Holiness: Its Nature, Hindrances, Difficulties, and Roots* (Peabody, MA: Hendrickson, 2007 reprint), p.195.

Chapter 11 — Back to Bethlehem (3:14-18)
1. A. S. Horne, *Torchbearers of the Truth: Sketches of the Scottish Covenanters* (Scottish Reformation Society, 1969), p.90.
2. The spelling has been modernized.

Chapter 12 — The courtroom scene (4:1-12)
1. The ESV names him three times in the verse, but the original Hebrew only has it twice.
2. J. Currid, *Study Commentary on Deuteronomy* (Darlington: Evangelical Press, 2006), p.244.

Chapter 13 — The descendant (4:13-22)
1. *Westminster Larger Catechism*, Question 12.